LET'S Re-GREAT BRITAIN

FUKP

PUB LANDLORD

AL MURRAY

LET'S Re-GREAT BRITAIN

MICHAEL JOSEPH
an imprint of
PENGUIN BOOKS

PENGUIN BOOKS

UK | USA | Canada | Ireland | Australia
India | New Zealand | South Africa
NOT Europe

Penguin Books is part of the Penguin Random House group of companies
whose addresses can be found at global.penguinrandomhouse.com.

First published 2015
001

This book is printed by Clays Ltd, St Ives plc of Bungay on behalf
of Penguin Random House Limited of 80 Strand, London, England.
It is published for the sole purpose of making loads of money and
is not intended to promote the electoral prospects of its author
[or any other dickhead].

Set in 10.5/16 pt Lucida Sans Std
Typeset by Mark Rowland
Poster design by Unreal-uk.com
Photography by Pete Dadds
Printed in Great Britain by Clays Ltd, St Ives plc

A CIP catalogue record for this book is
available from the British Library

ISBN: 978–1–405–92210–4

www.greenpenguin.co.uk

MIX
Paper from
responsible sources
FSC® C018179

Penguin Random House is committed to a
sustainable future for our business, our readers
and our planet. This book is made from Forest
Stewardship Council® certified paper.

*To Mum, Dad, Carlsberg and
Ramrod the Dog*

CONTENTS

FOREWORD

by **Sir Winston Churchill**, 1874–1965, via Sally Morgan, TV Psychic

I once said, when in corporeal, human form, before my soul slipped the heavy bonds of mortal gravity, that 'democracy is the worst form of government, except for all those other forms that have been tried from time to time'. Though I say so myself, it is good, is it not? Indeed, it is just the sort of quote someone might use at the start of a book about politics and democracy.

Here in Elysium, where there is no Parliament and the Almighty rules without so much as a select committee, there is time to watch and observe the state of things in the Mother of Parliaments, the United Kingdom. And what is clear from my place on this delightful cloud, where often I play chess with, amongst others, Mr Gandhi – few of my other earthly contemporary politicians seem to be here, they are perhaps in the Other Place; Mr Gandhi plays a lively game of chess but doesn't really put up a fight – is that those who stand as custodians to this proud tradition have let things slip somewhat.

— 1 —

The country has dined on an indigestible meal, a bland diet of a succession of men – and women! – who have dwindled ever smaller, who pay less and less attention to the people they seek to represent, who seem to be squandering the great freedoms fought for by men and women during my estimable time. Blood, Toil, Tears and Sweat have no place in this gluten-free republic! This kind of politics is the very thing up with the British people shall not put!

Fortunately, one man has come, one man prepared to tell it, as he says, 'like it is'. A man who has sought my endorsement from the next world. This audacity, this action, offers you a measure of him and his philosophy, his readiness to go further than those around him. He is a man I would be happy to call 'Guv'nor'.

'I also have spoken to your grandpa, who misses you greatly, and says watch out for your new boyfriend – he is not The One.'

INTRO:

CAN YOU TELL ME WHERE MY COUNTRY LIES?

This is the greatest country in the world. Make no mistake. Yes it is. Maybe I should say that again, it doesn't get said enough after all. **This is the greatest country in the world**. But we have to be frank: currently we've lost our way. We are on the edge of a precipice by the edge of a cliff next to a crevasse beside a crack next to a hole. Men and women up and down these fair isles of ours are in despair. Some days it feels like the whole world is falling in on us.

Even then, **this is the greatest country in the world**. Which makes you wonder what abroad might be like. No wonder they're all coming over here. More on that later.

But while remaining the greatest country in the world it is also in the shit. In fact it might be said that we are **up Shit Creek without a paddle**.

Consider that. We say it often enough but have you stopped to think it through?

Being **up Shit Creek without a paddle**, I mean. If you were to go up Shit Creek you'd take at least one spare paddle, at least one pair of gloves, wet wipes, spray bleach, clothes pegs. But the paddle is the thing you'd need most to stop you drifting down Shit Creek and into Diarrhoea Lake or wherever. You wouldn't want to paddle with your hands, which is the situation we are in. Your nice little boating trip has gone awry, and now you're drifting up Shit Creek and need to decide whether to eat your packed lunch first or start paddling with your hands on an empty stomach. And even if you did have wet wipes you wouldn't get all the shit from Shit Creek off your hands once you'd taken your gloves off. And some of it would have splashed on to the Clingfilm on the sandwich. Who'd want to be in that position?

Well right now the UK is deciding whether to **paddle with its hands in the shit** or **eat its sandwich first**. What kind of decision is that to have to make? But that is where we have found ourselves thanks to the powers that be.

Now, don't get me wrong. There is lots that is right with this country.

We are current **World War Champions of the World**, we have an undisputed thousand-year clean sheet. We haven't lost a war for over a thousand years, and it has been most heartening to see the RAF back in the saddle in recent months over Iraq, showing the world who's boss with our two jets and that drone we bought in Maplin's.

There's more to be cheerful about too. In other countries **poor people starve to death.** Ours don't: in fact we have some of the **fattest poor people in the world**. Instead of starving to death they gorge themselves on chips until their hearts explode. **Take pride**.

Not only that, we have bigger units of measurement than they do in Europe. The inch – two and a half times the size of a centimetre. A mile – one and a half kilometres, at least.

'SKY TELLY IS A HUMAN RIGHT.'

And who can forget the **Olympics in 2012**? Obviously that was quite a while ago, but there's no country that lobs doubles of its monarch out of a helicopter with as much style as the UK. That glorious summer seems so long ago now, the memory tarnished, the golden postboxes long forgotten. And anyway it cost a bloody fortune.

But a great deal has gone wrong lately. People feel like the political classes are in it for themselves and don't care about them. Expenses scandals have left us feeling ripped off. These people who want a free lunch and expect a lifetime of handouts? Do these people really represent us?

The mainstream parties have sold this country down the river to their fat-cat buddies who dodge their taxes and then there's the big corporations blah blah blah multinationals blah blah blah dialectical blah blah blah Occupy blah blah blah capitalism is bad blah blah blah.

We are also up against a European Communist superstate that, no longer content with trying to straighten bananas and abolish the ounce, right now is using the internet to zoom in on the unborn children of the UK and teach them French and metric [check this please, Steve] using the **CERN giant Hardon Super Collider** (that's what it's really for) while still in the womb. **Back off, Brussels.**

And worst of all, there's the embarrassing spectacle of the flood of immigrants coming over to this country:

hard-working, cheap, some of them have even got the fucking nerve to be qualified doctors and nurses, doing the sort of work we'd do if we could be arsed but can't. Is this what William the Conqueror, Richard the Lionheart, the Duke of Marlborough, Admiral Nelson, the Duke of Wellington, Private Hook and Lady Di died for?

And then there's the travesty of human rights. Who in their right mind wants Muslamic Fundamentaloid terror suspects to have access to jet-packs? Yeah, exactly, but it seems that faceless Europrats*† are determined to ensure that portable low-level atmospheric flight equipment for people who want to destroy our way of life is some kind of inalienable right. And **where's my jet-pack**? Why don't I get one? **Is this the future we were promised?**

Of course it isn't. And it's not the future we deserve either.

And that is why it is time for **Common Sense** to prevail. And why it's time for some **Common Sense** thinking on politics.

Honest about making the kind of promises no one could keep

---

*Might trademark that, actually: T-shirts, mugs. Think of the money the Keep Calm & Carry On bloke made.
†Oh yes, this book contains footnotes.

WHY POLITICS?

One of the penalties for refusing to participate in politics is that you end up being governed by your inferiors. Plato

Cheers, Plato. You got that right. Messed up on the Platonic relationship thing though.

Politics is, they say, **show business for ugly people**. You'll have heard that one and you might think it's both funny and wise – and indeed you might take a look at the current crop of politicians and say yes, yes it is. Then again you might be someone who watches TV, say *EastEnders*, and think in that case why aren't these people in the cabinet?

But before you read too much into it, the 'they' who say this by the way are journalists, and journalism is show business for curious, amoral, perverted, venal and slippery people who won't bat an eyelid before they go through your bins or hack your phones, and that's before we get on to what they look like. So let's not get too bothered about what they say about politics.

You might think – as a regular person who's not

bothered by any of this, or at least views the best way to handle things that stink so bad is by holding them at arm's length, possibly over a bin while pinching your nose – along the lines of the **Third Rule of Common Sense*** which as we all know is:

'How Does This Affect Me?'

After all, the best thing about politics these days is that, even though it grinds on day in, day out, it only pops up in the news for maybe three or four minutes and then vanishes again. You might not even notice it if you're lucky. If you don't buy a newspaper you might never run into it. But even though you might not be all that bothered, the whole time there are people

*The three rules of Common Sense are outlined in a previous book of mine for another publisher whom I won't mention. Common Sense comprises three component parts: 1) Knowledge; 2) Think It Through; and 3) How Does This Affect Me?

dedicating their entire lives to it, people who live, eat, breathe and sleep it. God knows what their breath is like and we shall not dwell on how their shit might smell. But because it's completely avoidable you'd be totally fine asking what it might have to do with you.

Trouble is, it affects everything. It didn't use to. Well, not much.

In the old days – before the First World War, which we won, no help from no one else – the government couldn't really do that much, hardly taxed you etc. You might go to school, you might go to the post office but that was about it. There weren't even any licensing laws.

Admittedly, ordinary folk didn't have the vote either, but in lots of ways that looks at this distance of a century like a fair trade. But then Germany decided it wanted to take these precious liberties off us, and the government had armies to fill with men and to pay for. This meant more taxes, but in return more votes. Votes bought with the blood, sweat and tears of heroes, even though they weren't actually fighting for that.

But: as a result the government shoved its nose quite thoroughly into everything. **Blame the Germans. Again.**

Promising a future without promises

Anyway, even though politics has the good grace not to take up too much of our time, and you might be one of those sensible enough to wave it away with the back of your hand like it was a lazy bumblebee while studying the form at Cheltenham, some people are increasingly pissed off with it.

However: contrary to **Common Sense**, they seem to think the answer is to have more of it. More politics. I ask you.

More politics? Are you bonkers mental?

Now: I put it to you – where is the logic in that? That was a rhetorical question by the way; you don't have to answer it. I mean, you can, but it won't help and it won't stop me from continuing with the point I was going to make. Keep up.*

Here's the point: if something is terrible, if something is letting you down, if something doesn't have the potential to please anyone, if it leaves you feeling short changed, left out, ignored, taken for granted, unheard, sullied, exploited, then why would you want to have even more of it? (This is not unlike the conversation I have with my regulars about their marriages most nights of the week.)

*It's OK, this might be the first book you ever read, and maybe also the last. But together we can do this.

Now, I'd counsel my regular drinkers that the one way to deal with a bad marriage is to grow a beard, get yourself a false passport and vanish. That or make sure the other party is properly insured. Honestly, though, the best solution to a bad marriage is often to hang on in there and maybe take up your own hobbies. The relationship between the UK and the EU has been described as a bad marriage: in that regard maybe the UK could spend more time in the shed restoring its economy or something, while the rest of Europe does Book Club.

But the problem with politics boils down like this.

Mammoth problems

There's two modes of complaint about politics and these have been with us since time began, since the first caveman was talked into moving to a new stretch of savannah and found that the mammoths weren't as bountiful as the Head-Man had led him to believe. He thought to himself, 'For whatever's in the sky's sake I've dragged my wife here bloody miles by her hair . . .' (the surviving social fragment of this, of course, is the eternal words 'no love, I'll drive') '. . . and now there's no mammoths, thanks a bunch. That's the last time I listen to you.'

Tax Evasion: Never has so much been owed by so few to so many

But did he demand the formation of a mammoth committee? Or the root-and-branch reform of the Head-Man's mammoth forecasting policy? Or an investigation into new mammoth hunting techniques? No, he did his own thing and hunted the bountiful elk instead. Actually, I don't know. We'll never know because it's impossible to know what they said or did because they didn't write it down, so whenever you read something like this the best thing to do is make that tooth sucking noise you sometimes hear on the bus coming from behind you and wonder what's happening.*

There's every chance he took a rock and smashed the Head-Man's brains out with it. And did that solve anything? Well, we'll never know that either, but it does sound like it might have. Simpler times. These options are no longer available to us. I'd keep those thoughts to yourself if I were you.

From [A] and [B]

Anyway: the two modes of complaint are what? That's where you were you dozy sod. Well – people are either saying:

✗ [A] 'why won't the government do something about this??!??!!!!' (and they always say it with that

---

*This is why museums should be free, because most of what's in them is made-up bollocks.

many exclamation marks and question marks and sometimes they hold up a banner saying something like that too). This sort of complaint makes governments twitchy and nervous and do nothing.

Or they say:

✗   [B] 'why have the government made such a mess of that???!!!????!!' and wave placards bearing said demand. This sort of stuff makes governments twitchy and nervous and do nothing.

Now it was, I believe, Alice in Wonderland who said she liked to hold two impossible breakfasts in the morning or something, and I may be nothing more than

a humble publican, who's only ever pulled pints, sorted snacks, dealt with single-entry book-keeping, drunks, fools, eejits and run a low-level scam on a fruit machine that doesn't work properly, but I can see and no doubt you can too that there is an immediate problem with these two demands.

After all, let's say the government do do something about this, like it says on placard [A]. And then they mess it up. The way that you and I know they do, from time to time (by time to time I mean all the time, of course). Then as sure as Ant follows Dec – though it could be the other way round; I'll be honest, I was long ago resigned to the fact I'll never know which one is which – the people with placard [B] will be out in force. Then they demand that the very people who made a mess of something should not just sort it out but then *carry on* doing stuff.

Or, if you boil it down to something simple: the bloke who cooked you that terrible dinner you complained about has been told to go away and cook you another terrible dinner. **Even though AND because** he cooked you a terrible dinner.

So what do you do? What is the solution? It could be argued that the very best thing a government could do is nothing, but that time is past. We live in the age of 'something must be done' and 'look busy' as the two main tenets of modern government. Governments would rather look busy doing something half arsed than simply leaving well alone. And if you do nothing, no matter how wise doing nothing might be, it'll make you look like you don't care. And how things look – well – nine-tenths of the law, innit? So again, what do we do about it?

Still, before you can pronounce on politics, of course, you need to read a lot of stuff, watch the news, read the papers, argue with politicians (bellowing at the telly counts), go to meetings, argue with the sad-sacks canvassing on your high street or the wannabe MP on your doorstep. Now: working in a pub affords a man all of these opportunities. And also, here's the thing: in a democracy – even a cobbled-together, held-together-with-Sellotape-and-chewing-gum democracy like the one we've got here in the UK that also happens to be the best one in the world by a considerable distance thank you very much – we are all participants. All of us.

Deny it all you like: but we are all equally qualified to have an opinion.
And have it listened to.
Even if it's mental rubbish.
So: hear me out, I say.
Fuck it, you bought the book, didn't you?

In this book I will put forward some solutions that should, without a doubt, make the country work better than ever. Because although it's a total fucking mess,

this is the greatest country in the world. Imagine what it must be like living anywhere else.

They say politics is the art of the possible. Well, I say we can do better than that. Politics should be the art of the impossible. It should make us all able to follow our dream, to live that dream, to be the dream we want to dare to dream (or something; this slogan needs work).

'Tomorrow is in the future.'

So: we start with Economics, because that's what you have to do these days. Bear with me.

TERMS OF GREETING

Any movement worth its salt has a term of greeting. And we adherents of the **Common Sense** movement should be no exception. However, most of the good ones have been used up. **Comrade**, that's gone, **Brother** can't be used for everyone, of course, its cousin **Bro** is one of the words we aim to ban, **Mate** – well Russell Brand has gone for that one but he says it like you say it to someone you've bumped into in the street, which is of course the only time you should say it if you're not Australian ('Sorry, mate').

Obergrüppenführer has sadly been tarnished by the events of the 1930s and 40s. So that is why we friends in **Common Sense** will call each other **SQUIRE**.

Because one day the whole country will accept FUKP

ECONOMICS

In the long run we are all dead.   J. M. Keynes

All You Ever Need To Know About **Economics,** Squire, roll up roll up.

Here's all you need to know about **Economics**. God it's hard to get this bit started. Because you and I know this is the bit when we glaze over. And the only people who can deal with it – look what it does to them, the state of **Robert Peston**, eh?

The thing is, it didn't use to matter. No one used to even know Economics existed. No one talked about it, no one cared. And it's not like gravity, which was there all along. Because you can't interfere with gravity and make gravity go wrong the way you can with **Economics**. **Economics** and economic policy fall very neatly under **Maradona's Law**: just because you can do something doesn't mean you should do something. Bastard. Never forget.

Basically it's all down to a bloke called **Karl Marx**. Now, youngsters may not have heard of him, or, worse still, they might have, but he was for quite a while one of the most important men in the world, though this only happened long after he'd shuffled off this mortal. And by 'most important man in the world' I mean in terms of ideas, not whether they'd take his picture leaving a restaurant or doing bloody selfies on a red carpet and that.

Marx had a really big idea. Yeah, I know what you're thinking, it was a **Bright Idea**, wasn't it? And we don't like **Bright Ideas**, do we? Well, no, no we don't, and this particular **Bright Idea** was no exception.

Marx's Bright Idea

Basically, he decided that the best way to view the world was through the prism of **Economics**, and that **Economics** and how it all works and unfolds has the answers in it, the answers to the present and the answers to how the future was going to work out. This, in turn, led to a thing called **Marxism** (and you know you're doing well if you get an -ism named after you, almost up there with having a disease named after you), which in turn tried its damnedest to turn into **Communism**.

Marx had done a lot of properly hard thinking, he had a big beard and clearly spent a great deal of time stroking it, and although he hadn't ever really had a proper job, he had a firm grip on what the working classes wanted and could look forward to once the revolution had come. Good man; having an imagination is important.

Ring-fencing the valuable British fencing industry

Karl Marx lived in London and, like most people who live in London, he ended up hating it. Fair enough. If one place was to lead a man to wanting the world to pull together and share and share alike it would be London, with its huge and annoying population of **knuckleheads**, **dopes**, **maroons** and **prats**. He hated London so much he wrote a book about the place, *Das Capital*, which contained an economic theory guaranteed to wreck the city. I know what you're thinking, he'd have made a great Mayor of London.

Marx was convinced he was right and as a result *Das Capital* ended up being a really thick book about it. The kind of thick book that no one ever really gets all the way through, but that doesn't actually matter, especially if you are also really thick, because all you really have to do is say you've read it and then you can get on with agreeing with each other on **who you're going to string up when the revolution comes**.

Ism-gasm

Now, the thing is, while he might have gone down as just another dreamer, Marx convinced loads of other

— 23 —

people he was right – and that takes some doing with a thick book about Economics – and so a whole load of people decided they were **Marxists** and set about trying to convince everyone else they wanted to be **Marxists** too and that it was for their own good. Marxists of course are not to be confused with **Leninists**, **Trotskyists**, **Stalinists** and **Communists**, who are all exactly the same no matter what they might tell you.*†‡§ This of course upset the people who didn't want to be **Marxists** and that ladies and gentlemen is the history of the Twentieth Century in a nutshell if that's how you happen to look at it.

It's much more complicated than that, obviously, but we haven't got all day. I'm not going to waste my or your time arguing over it. And anyone worth their ready salted knows that Stalin was a total murderous bastard, Mao a hideous murdering prick, and Pol Pot – make no mistake – a thunder-cunt who was into murder. All done in the name of Marx's precious revolution. Endless stringings-up, starvings, shootings, incarceratings, purges – you name it, the revolution required it. No amount of 'they've been

---

*Lenin: Russian bloke, pointy beard, trouble
†Trotsky: Russian bloke, bushy 'tache, trouble
‡Stalin: Russian bloke, luxury 'tache, trouble
§Communists: various facial hair stylings, trouble.

misrepresented by the other side' stuff will paper over those cracks, will it? It's like the bloke who slaps his wife – he can buy as many rounds as he likes but no one will ever lend him their lawnmower.

But the thing is, Karl Marx knew for sure the way the world was going, and he knew it with great certainty, the kind that would mean you'd not invite him out for a pint more than once. I mean really, who wants their drinking disturbed with all that stuff about the **dialectic** between the **bourgeoisie** and the **proletariat**? The inevitable rise of the working classes to take possession of the means of production etc? Not me. But, unfortunately, because he'd used Economics to come up with this theory of the century, everyone has to now take Economics seriously, when previously what they'd worried about was whether the king was an inbred dribbling idiot or a Catholic and/or both.* (They went together as often as not.)

If we are honest, what Marx really did was extend the idea of getting your round in, so you can hardly blame him for trying.

But how did Karl Marx know all this? He knew it because **he had reckoned it**.

*It's something worth knowing that the history of this country as often as not has been down to whether the King or Queen is a Catholic or not, or whether they fancied Catholics or not. God help us.

The basis of all Economics

A lot of baloney gets said about **Economics** and it's certainly been talked up to the point where you can be an expert in it and go on the telly and point at a graph. (Like Russell Brand, I'm no fan of graphs either, but there we are, we live in a world with graphs and people use them to communicate and persuade. Graphs, like quinoa,* can't be uninvented.)

Yes, Squire, they're good at churning out tables as well as graphs, and my God they've got some major jargon going on.

Are you drinking what we're drinking?

Check out **this lot**: [I've helped out here as best I can]

> **Absolute advantage**: can you make it for less than the other guy?
> **Assets**: tits, boobs, jugs. (Old school.)
> **Balance of trade**: have you sold more or less to the other guy?
> **Barter**: swapshop, basically.
> **Bond**: your promise to pay the other guy. Sometimes people buy these promises off you, so

*Inca for 'muck'.

they can promise to pay the other guy. God knows why they'd want to do that.

Change in demand: imagine – you have to study at uni for three years to figure out what this means, for pity's sake.

Change in supply: see above.

Circular flow of goods and services: I give the money to him, he gives the money to me, I give the money to him, he gives the money to me.

Collateral: how much you've got tied up in that house you can't sell.

Cost: completely different from price, value or worth or any of those things that might seem to be pretty much the same thing.

Credit: we'll get into this later.

Decision making: that's a whole term at Cambridge, mate.

Deficit: fuck me, if I never hear this word again I shall run stark naked from London to Glasgow.

Deflation: the opposite of inflation, innit? No one has ever seen this happen, ever.

Economic wants: what the other guy wants and how you can sort it.

Entrepreneur: French word! Given the state of the French economy, which is like a middle-aged man whose croissant-clogged arteries don't have the gumption to muster beyond the slightest semi despite a tourniquet made of red tape, it's a marvel this word so beloved of people who want to encourage business and go it alone and all that and drive a second-hand 3 series Beemer, comes from France.

Exchange rates: the thing propping up airport bureaux de change all over the world. I will explain why below, though, fear not.

Exports: not, as you might imagine, lagers with a strength of at least 1 per cent more than their common-or-garden cousins, but the stuff that gets shipped out of the country.

FTSE: come on admit it, no one knows what this is. It's on the news every night, every night they report on how it's doing and in front rooms up and down the country regular people shrug and wonder what it means. When it goes up too much the people who know what it is panic, and when it goes down the same people panic as well, though if we're honest they panic more about the latter.

GDP (Gross domestic product): This one is pretty obvious, it means the total amount that the country produces. In total. Before expenses, takeaways, cabs home etc. Apparently there's a version called GDP, real, which is that amount adjusted for inflation but it's too depressing so they never read that one out.

Human resources: those fuckers in HR who sacked Reg, the old bloke just before his full pension kicked in, who was the only person in the place who knew what he was doing and now you're all flying blind.

Loss: move on please.

Market: there are two kinds of market, the one

you and I know, where you buy knock-off DVDs, socks and spuds in large amounts, and the 'markets', who usually won't stand for something: whatever it is, the markets won't like it.

National debt: how much the country owes. It may seem strange, despite taxing us left right centre in and out of the wazoo and even VAT on fucking chips, the country has to borrow money to get by too. Why? Is the UK hooked on the gee-gees? Does HM Govt have a crack problem? I don't know. But somehow apparently we are up to our necks in debt. Not that it's the money we owe from the Second World War – we paid that off in 2009 or something. By the going down of the sun, we shall remember the rates of interest.

Price: completely different from cost, value, worth, RRP or any of those things that might seem to be pretty much the same thing.

Profit: the only interesting bit. What's left after all the other crap. Less than you'd think.

Standard of living: never enough, basically. No matter who you are. Human nature, innit?

Stocks and shares: the horses for posh people. Who have the horses too; only difference is, they can afford them.

Surplus: when there's too much of the thing you're trying to shift, like the great pork scratching glut of 2002.

Trade: you pay me, I give it to you. Or I pay you, you give it to me. Simple. What could possibly go wrong? Yet when Chinese Fred comes into the snug bar selling hams apparently that isn't trade, it's theft.

Unemployment: more on that later.

Work: more on that later (that's right, smart arse, like any proper job I'm putting it off 'til later).

There are loads more of these, many of which have clearly been designed to fend off the likes of you and me. And fair enough, that's what any bunch of experts do when they want to stop people from listening. If I get started on draught-flow systems and snack management, or mention BPW (barrels per week), the thing I'm really trying to do is either a) get you to eff off or b) make sure you don't know what I'm on about but nod along anyway and accept what a top fella I must be for knowing all this.

Economists use this trick all the time, and the reason they do is because they have to. And they have to because they have succeeded in getting everyone barking up their particular wrong tree, a tree upon which money doesn't grow (they don't exist, no matter what Ed Miliband might tell you) but **total bollocks** instead.

Stopping the rot before the rot stops you

Names matter

Besides, they had to change the name of **Economics** for one simple reason – it was a bit obvious and folks might figure out what was going on. Its original name back in the time of alchemy and all that was **Reckonomics**.

Because that's what it actually consists of, people reckoning stuff. Oh yes, you can go to university and study it for three years, go on to do a doctorate, go on the telly and baffle everyone with your understanding of graphs and that, but the truth is all it actually consists of is looking at the figures and saying, '**Yeah I reckon it'll go up this week**.'

'You know it makes Common Sense'

This, I reckon – and here's the fun part, Reckonomics means you can reckon anything – explains why the boys and girls who work in the City are paid so handsomely. Because in the end they're guessing and if they fuck it up they're done for. You want me to make a billion-pound punt – pay me properly, you bastards. I don't want the responsibility, it's hard enough coming up with a proper price on a pint that doesn't upset everyone. Believe me – you can't please both the punters and the brewery on that one. Ever. Or HMRC if you take matters into your own hands.

Once you've cracked the Reckonomic nut the whole thing becomes a lot clearer. You can see why it all works the way it does. Things carry on happily with, say, a bank* reckoning it can carry on lending money to a business that reckons it'll do fine the next couple of years. No one knows for sure if it will, they just reckon they probably will. Or might. Maybe. Then when it becomes clear they reckoned wrong they reckon it's time for the company to pay up and that's that. The day of reckoning.

But what this all rotates around and relies upon is **Credit** too. And what is Credit? Well. I can tell you what it *isn't*, for starters.

Credit: it's not what you think it is

Credit – what is it? We have all run into it. Some of us might be struggling with it, but what actually is it?

Well one thing it isn't is what the banks and building societies want us to think it is. **Borrowing**. Credit bears no resemblance to borrowing.

---

*Not a proper bank, mind, one of those banks that has a name like KGML and doesn't have a cashpoint machine. Not a proper bank.

You have a best mate. He asks you if he can **borrow** your football. You say yes. You lend him the football. A couple of months later you say, 'Here, mate, can I have that football back I lent you?' He says all right. And he gives your football back. What he doesn't have to do is give you **three and a half footballs back**.

And that's borrowing. What you do when you borrow money from the bank isn't borrowing. What you do is you buy the bloody stuff. And they try to make out you're borrowing the stuff off them, like they're doing you some kind of favour, but no one ever came and took your house off you if you didn't give them their football back. If you want to borrow five hundred quid from the bank you have to pay them back twelve hundred quid. That seven hundred pound difference is called **Interest** and the reason it's called **Interest** is because if you were making that kind of profit on five hundred quid you'd be **Interested**.

Buying you drinks with your money

So what actually is Credit? Well, the word is as good a place to start as any. It comes from the Latin – get me, a regular Boris Johnson – from the Latin word *credo*, meaning *I believe*. Because that's how it works, it's a belief system.

Now immediately we can all see there's a problem there. People believe all sorts of stuff. Mad stuff. E.g.:

- ✗ They believe the Americans put a man on the moon. If it was worth going we would have gone first, in a boat. Besides, we had the NHS to pay for.
- ✗ Some people believe that *On Her Majesty's Secret Service* is the best Bond film and they believe that makes them unique.
- ✗ People believe that JFK* was assassinated by the KGB, the CIA and the Mafia by getting one of his Secret Service men's guns to go off by accident. Nonsense. It was suicide.

It gets worse, and more relevant:

- ✗ You believe you're going to pay off your Credit card.
- ✗ The Bank believes you're going to pay off your mortgage.

And that's the problem with Credit. It works as long as everyone believes the same thing. In fact you can owe them tons of money, hundreds of thousands on a mortgage, but as long as they believe you, you can carry on. The moment they don't believe you, you end up in:

Debt: Credit's evil twin

And what is **Debt**? Look at it carefully. That unnecessary **b**. Well, it's **Doubt**, isn't it? Debt is what happens to you when the bank no longer believes you. Their Credit, their belief in you, has gone and all of a sudden you

*The youngest man ever to have lived.

owe them money. Suddenly the money they were perfectly happy you owing them they want back. It's like having a hangover while you're drinking. Well I think it is. Not sure exactly.

You have to hand it to the banks and the rest of them: they've got us by the short and curlies and we keep coming back for more. Smooooooooth moves. No wonder they pay themselves so much. They're smart people.

But basically this is how the whole of the world's financial system works:

- ✗ What people reckon: **ECONOMICS**
- ✗ People believing it: **CREDIT**
- ✗ Right up to the point when they don't believe it any more: **DEBT**

So as you can see, a lot of this is pretty simple when you strip it down to its basics.

London gets trading on a Monday morning, the lads have a look at the *Financial Times*, they look at Monday morning's figures and they say to themselves, using Economics, 'Yeah I reckon it's going to go up.' They go to their boss and say, 'Here, Guv, we reckon it's going to go up today.' He says, 'OK, thanks, chaps, I'll call my brother, he works at the bank, he'll believe me, he'll give us the money,' and so off they go, and the market becomes confident and onwards and upwards and that. Then **Frankfurt** calls **London**, to find out what London reckons, they believe what **London** reckons and their stock market goes up and so on around the world and up it goes. **Tokyo** calls **Frankfurt** and so on. This carries on until suddenly they stop believing what they've been reckoning and the whole thing falls in on itself and Ireland finds itself in the shit again.

The main difference between the world of global finance and borrowing a couple of hundred quid in your local is the menaces are more personal. And this leads us to

THE DEFICIT.

THE DEFICIT

Debt is a social and ideological construct, not a simple economic fact.   Noam Chomsky

Thanks Noam, but the bailiffs didn't really go for that and took my telly. Everyone else

Right, I'm going to say right now and without hesitation that after five years of the **ConDem** government I still don't know what the **Deficit** is. I'll bet that no one does. All we know is we have to get it down. Apparently.

So how would I do that if it was up to me? Well, there are some good ideas out there and in the spirit of true democracy I have no qualms about stealing the other parties' ideas and passing them off as my own.

George best

I very much like the way little **George Osborne*** has gone about it, by borrowing more so he can pay it off. That takes style, panache, imagination and most of all bullshit. In all honesty I don't think he's been given

Because somehow has to

*Small bloke, of course he's a Borrower.

enough credit for pulling that off over the last five years or so. One day in the future he'll be in one of those believe-it-or-not-type books alongside the bloke who **sold Tower Bridge dressed as an Arab**. Or Jeffrey Archer.

It's quite the trick. But you can see how it might happen. You think, 'Sod it, I'll only borrow what I need for this month,' and then you forget, don't you, and the bills pile up and you think, 'Ah well, I'll borrow some more.' And precisely BECAUSE the menaces are less personal, there's no Big Dave threatening to bust one of your ankles and your wing mirrors aren't getting smashed every time you park outside the Red Lion, you just carry on borrowing. And that's what George has done, bless him.

This kind of brass neck tells you a lot about George Osborne. For one thing it makes you warm to the guy. A fella like that would be able to get you out of any scrape; no matter how bad, he'd come up with something, open that strange little squished mouth of his and go for it. The lad's got balls, that's what I'm saying. Now I know folk like to say he's out of touch with the real world, doesn't know how ordinary people live, and I don't doubt that for a second. In fact I would bet my bottom dollar that he's never driven a forklift for cash only because he's got a bad back.

However. This strategy of borrowing more to pay off the deficit can only end in disaster, but obviously the idea is for it to end in disaster when the next lot get in. Nice moves, George. Which means whatever appalling, shattered, bankrupt, running on empty, up to our eyeballs in debt and generally done for state the economy is in, you're going to have to stop and admire his footwork.

We must take our medicine (not all at once)

Ed, Balls

Look, there is a very real problem here and it's not my fault. In fact it's nobody's fault, not even his. **Ed Balls** is called **Ed Balls** and that is just the way the universe has gone and turned things out, destined since the Big Bang or whatever that right now there'd be a bloke called **Ed Balls** and we would have to take him seriously. Why now? Why now, when the most important general election for a generation is facing us, when **Common Sense** has at last a chance to storm the barricades – though hopefully without having to put too much effort into it, thanks – does one of the main protagonists involved have to be called **Balls**?

What this proves is that Fate laughs in the faces of us all, not just the Great and Good (I'm not including him in that, by the way, be reasonable) but in the faces of everyone. And it is a good enough reason for us to discount everything he says, for **Ed Balls** represents the utter futility of human existence. Whatever he might get up there and tell us, his name is Balls, the universe is mocking us, give up, what's the point of anything at all? Just as Fate served us up Winston Churchill at the precise moment when we and the rest of the world needed him, this time Fate is chucking up a huge cosmic joke for us to all chew on.

This is surely **his cosmic function**, his true destiny, his Kismet, if you will, above and beyond whatever ambitions he may have as a politician. It's as if he has been sent, sent from another world, not unlike Superman, sent to remind us all that the world is absurd, there's no point to anything much, that you're better off laughing it all off with a shrug and saying to yourself '**Ed Balls**'.

The next time you miss your flight: '**Ed Balls**'.

The next time the dog shits in the kitchen: '**Ed Balls**'.

The next time your wife packs her bags and goes to her mum's: '**Ed Balls**'.

The next time you tread on Lego tiptoeing through a kid's room and howl, waking the baby: '**Ed Balls**' and it'll all go away.

You'll realize nothing really matters, there's no point

reaching for the stars when there's a universe with **Ed Balls** in it. Try it: '**Ed Balls**'.

Anyway. What does Mr Balls have to offer? Well, he's consistent, I'll give him that. It's all about bankers' bonuses. Whatever it is he's going to pay for it out of bankers' bonuses AND he's going to ban them. Joined-up thinking. The lad's a genius.

Also: **Ed Balls*** has said that the government have cut stuff too much and nowhere near enough. I think. The thing is, it doesn't matter, because what's going to happen if he becomes Chancellor is whatever appalling, shattered, bankrupt, running on empty, up to our eyeballs in debt and generally done for state the economy is in, people will be able to shrug and say to themselves '**Ed Balls**' and none of it will matter quite so much. Thank God for the cosmos eh?

Danny Alexander

What, really? You want to know what I think about him? Come off it. Besides, we have plans for Danny. Basically he's George Osborne's personal gimp-toy. How the mighty party of, er, David Steel and, um, the other one you know the . . . I can't remember oh Christ no not Cyril Smith Jesus . . . has fallen. As it happens I have no idea what he's done regarding the deficit, though what

*'**Ed Balls**'.

I will take from his stance is that no one having the faintest idea what you're up to and who you are makes it very hard for people to point the finger.

The others

No one else seems to talk about the deficit much: the SNP up in Scotland, which decided to stay in the UK, though stone me you'd never know judging by the way some of them are banging on about it right now, hardly seem to mention it. **Like it's someone else's problem.** I think the SNP were going to plant some money trees, maybe, that or rely on the oil price going up for ever. **What you do have to admire about their campaign last year is they kept it vague.**

Vague is good, you can't argue with vague. Try it.

'What time do you want lunch?'

'One-ish.'

You can try to disagree with that but it's lunchtime and because there's no specific time set you can't be late or early.

The Greens want to dismantle capitalism but they want to do it while smiling and being nice to people. They also want to make the country vegetarian, which means banning pork scratchings, **so they can do one,**

— 42 —

frankly. Do one, The Greens, do one. It's enough to make a man want to emigrate, except abroad is full of foreigners.

UKIP? Well, I don't know what they plan to do about the deficit. I reckon they'll have a look at what I'm proposing and copy that. Sigh. That's the risk you run when you're the voice of reason.

So, what would my **Guv'norment** do about the deficit (whatever that is)? I think the ideas below have a lot to be recommended:

1. Borrow more, but shred the paperwork having signed the Wonga form with my left hand.
2. Consolidate the country's debts into one manageable lump sum.
3. Plant money trees, especially up North.
4. Burn down the Houses of Parliament for the insurance.
5. Grow a beard, buy some heavy framed specs.
6. Leave the country.

This six-point plan by the looks of it is the only solution to the ongoing problem of the deficit, though I also pledge that before I do all this I'll find out what the deficit actually is and if it's really worth worrying about or whether it's just a way of looking like you're doing something useful when actually there are much bigger problems.

Everyone bangs on about the price of petrol, but what about the price of Maltesers? They now cost £50 a week.

Bruce Bucklesqueeze, 23, former Slimmer of the Year

OUR VISION FOR THE ECONOMY

A strong economy is the key to winning the Global Race.* That or performance-enhancing drugs, but I don't want the UK growing moobs from steroids or any of that, like France.

But there are measures we can take to boost the UK economy and return us to our status as **Number 1 Global Powerhouse** in buying tellies off the Chinese in the World.

✗ **Fracking**. There's been a lot of controversy about fracking the last few years. If they'd called it something more boring I'm sure no one would have noticed. But the UK's energy needs have to be addressed. For this reason I am all in favour of fracking everywhere except where I live. **Common Sense**.

✗ **FUKP will cut business rates to any business that will vote for us**. We haven't got

*This is something that David Cameron was banging on about for a while before he settled on his current strategy of saying: 'Look! Everybody! Ed Miliband!'

any backers currently, but, y'know, we're open to offers. Everyone else seems to have someone leaning on them asking them for some favour or other. I'm not saying we have no principles, just we haven't been bought any yet.

✗ Following up on our **extra ten pence in the pound** policy, **FUKP** will also make the little 5p piece be worth two quid every other Tuesday.

✗ The **Cost of Living Crisis** is something we need to tackle. Food Banks are a disgrace. The rate of interest on a tin of baked beans is something that shames the whole of Britain, we will increase that, no more extra helpings for food bank fat-cats.

✗ The fruit machine industry to be nationalized, all proceeds to be fed into paying off the deficit, **Common Sense**, harnessing the UK's gambling community, should have paid it off by next Christmas.

✗ The Eurozone crisis has had effects reaching far around the globe. It's got so bad the world is looking to the Germans for leadership and the French for moral courage. Remember, the pound by being worth more than one euro proves that the UK is worth more than the whole of Europe put together. The only solution is to **put Europe on the pound and rename it the British Empire**.

✗   Inequality is something that blights the lives of all. **FUKP** pledge that from 2030 no one will be taller than anyone else and everyone will have the same size feet.

FUKP: telling you the things we reckon you want to hear about the Economy.

'New Britain, new vision, new contact lenses'

Ain't no party like a FUKP party

HOW YOUR AVERAGE, TYPICAL, NORMAL MAN (OR WOMAN) IN THE STREET WOULD BE AFFECTED BY MY COMMON SENSE FINANCIAL POLICIES

✔ A divorced man called Kev with above average alcohol intake, lives in a bedsit, runs a clapped-out Nissan Micra, plays five-a-side once a week, thinks *Anchorman 2*'s brilliant, would be better off by 12.7 pints of lager (or 13 pints of bitter) per year.

✔ A man doing a minimum of twenty years for armed robbery, who lives in a 6ft x 8ft cell, would be two-and-a-half ounces of snout a year better off.

✔ A single man who's never had a girlfriend, lives with his parents, stays in his bedroom all day playing daft computer games and watching mucky films on the internet, would be 1.5 boxes of Kleenex a year better off.

✔ A married Chancellor of the Exchequer called 'George' who's currently on £134,565 a year **would be worse off by £134,565 a year**.

✔ A divorced Prince Andrew who lives in palaces, flies helicopters, plays golf and issues official denials to the media, would be better off (not my decision).

✔ A single woman with no children, and an income of £100,000 a year would be better off not going on dating sites – bunch of losers and weirdos, luv.

✔ A single domestic neutered cat with no kittens, living in a cosy basket, would be 5.7 food pouches a year better off.

✔ A married wasp with dependent larvae, living in a semi-detached nest would be better off by eleven half-empty glasses of shandy a summer.

FINANCE

What's in the Guv'nor's briefcase?

MENU

* IMPORTANT STUFF (NONE OF YOUR BUSINESS)

* LUCKY GONK

* WILLIAM HILL BIRO

* GINSTERS STEAK SLICE

* JUICY FRUIT

* POCKET CALCULATOR

* BEST FRIED CHICKEN & KEBAB FLYER

* 1 AAA BATTERY (DEAD)

* COPY OF *METRO* (2 JULY 2007)

* AERO (ONE PIECE)

* FLUFF

* BUMPER WORDSEARCH PUZZLE BOOK

* SCRATCHCARD

* PLASTIC FORK

AUSTERITY

The result in the recent Greek elections has sent out massive shockwaves – not only within the EU, but across the world. As a result of this, many questions have been raised, such as: does this spell the end for austerity in the West? How does this affect the Eurozone? And can I get the deposit back on that fortnight I booked in Faliraki?

In order for our economy to get back on its feet and the wheels of industry to begin going round and round once more, I've worked out that we're going to have to begin taking even worse-tasting medicine than George Osborne's been giving us these last five years. If his course of treatment constituted of a Junior Disprin washed down with orange squash, then what I prescribe is more along the lines of quadruple heart bypass surgery while the patient is still awake, root canal work, followed by a course of really painful physio by a big hairy-arsed geezer with cold hands.

Making plans for your money like it's someone else's

The Guv'nor's blueprint for recovery

✔ Make (and sell) more things, ideally at a profit.

✔ Reduce Eric Pickles by 40 per cent.

✔ Payday loan companies to be outlawed, and replaced by the traditional behind-the-bar slate system.

✔ Privatize snow.

✔ Taking offence to be taxed: anyone who is offended has to pay £1 a time. We'll be out of debt by Christmas, that or people will stop being offended about *EVERYTHING* – win–win.

✔ Autumn Statement would go back to being called 'The Budget' – because that's what it is.

✔ Add an additional month to the year to boost productivity, the UK with an extra month's accounts to submit will out-produce the rest of the world. New month to be called PoomBah.

✔ Wasps to be released in hospital wards to free up beds.

✔ People flying business class to shout 'Work harder!' at people in economy.

✔ Migrating birds to be charged on return to the UK.

✔ Severn Bridge toll charges in both directions. Fair's fair.

✔ Introduction of a national meat raffle.

✔ Something about quantatititive easing.

✔ Check spelling of quantatititive.

✔ Don't spend it all at once.

Together we can create new history

Decent honest hard working law abiding tax reasonable sensible down to earth normal reasonable rational calm straight forward no nonsense decent normal hard working down to earth sensible

WORK

Choose a job you love, and you will never have to work a day in your life. Confucius

Confucius said that. A philosopher who sat around all day looking out of the window.

Easy for him to say, layabout bastard. Foreign, too.

Work. We all know work. Such a small word for such a big thing.

The difference between working hard and hard work. We all know that.

We also know there's a sickie here, a sickie there to be taken. But we all know work matters, that work is important. That work is the thing we have to do, that it's how we define ourselves, shape our lives. And that it drives us mad. That we hate it. That it leaves us feeling trapped. Disappointed. Thwarted. Underpaid. Crushed. Can drive us to drink (I'm not going to knock that).

So when there's a few quid in not working, well, it's tempting, isn't it? I mean, you hate your boss, you're bored with your job. Why not? Stop at home, sign on. Jackpot. No need to get up in the morning, late start, watch a bit of TV, pop to the offie get some cans, go home, bit more TV. It sounds brilliant, doesn't it? Admit it, you're tempted. Nothing to do, nothing to drive you mad. No boss to get on your tits, no promotion to miss out on, no Christmas party to embarrass yourself at, no work mates to get off with.

No wonder millions of people opt for living this dream.

But we have to get Britain back to work. But how? Apart from everyone doing jobs for cash and not worrying too much about the paperwork and that. How do we teach kids the meaning of hard work? The value of graft?

- ✗ Urgently train up teams of Child Catcher-style worker-catcher teams.
- ✗ Weaponize Katie Hopkins.
- ✗ Shout in people's faces 'get a job for Christ's sake' but while smiling, caring.

But the real problem, as we all know, is that kids have the wrong role models.

Reality TV stars who've not done a day's work in their lives, the sort of people who go on 'journeys' by sitting around in a TV studio, the kind of people who cry twice and think that means they have a personality. Kids have no work ethic, they think they're entitled, they think they deserve stuff they haven't earned, you know the rest.

But there is a solution. A **Common Sense** one too. Simple.

✗ Pyramids. Dead simple, build a ring of pyramids around the M25, fifty of them.
✗ All kids between fifteen and eighteen have to work on this project, no excuses. Might weed out a few asthmatics.
✗ Fifty old-school Egyptian-style pyramids, made from 20–30,000 giant clay bricks that they have to drag on a piece of string while a bloke whacks them with a whip.
✗ Once the pyramids are completed, fifty reality TV stars will be selected by phone vote, killed on telly in a sort of live eviction special (this way the scheme will pay for itself, or wash its own face as people with an MBA might say).
✗ Each reality TV star wrapped in bog roll and put in an unmarked pyramid (last one to die gets a plaque).

That way we not only teach kids the meaning of hard work, we slay their false gods and save the future for future generations. Two birds, one stone. **Common Sense**.

Time for a change of barrels

THE GLORIOUS DEAD

And how to make the most of them

The United Kingdom's democracy was built upon the dead of two world wars.* Almost a million men from all over the British Empire and her Dominions in the First World War (which we won) and then about a quarter of a million in the Second World War (ditto).

This sacrifice is on a scale unimaginable these days. I think it's fair to say the modern news media wouldn't know what to do about it. They'd run a counter in the corner of the screen or something; the Battle of the Somme would have it spinning like your electricity meter when you've got a band playing in the Function Room. Lest we forget.

But the war dead hold a special place in politics, especially in the UK. They offer the politician two things, and you're a cack-handed fool if you don't make the most of both.

Ask not what your country can do for you, you selfish git

*And one World Cup. Sorry. It's a reflex.

— 61 —

1) Clinching an argument.

You can win almost any argument by wheeling out the war dead. Someone saying they don't want to vote? People died in a war for that, pal, watch it. The NHS? People fought and died for that, mate (after all, Hitler had famously said 'Ein Volk, ein Reich, no free health care at the point of delivery!'). It doesn't work for everything – say a parking dispute – but you never know, it might catch someone out if you say, 'Is this what the men on Anzio beach fought and died for?' Worth a punt, I guess.

But if you know what you're doing you can argue your way out of anything. They must be delighted to have gone to the front reassured that they'd get wankers off the hook day in, day out for over a century. But it's there and you'd be a fool not to use it. They did die for freedom of speech after all.

Bringing back shame

2) Acting all noble.

Modern politicians don't get many chances to appear noble or dignified. Ed Miliband knifing his brother – that was the end of his chances to come across as noble and principled. He's carried on blithely imagining that no one would think 'you little shit' for the rest of his political career. David Cameron trying to hug hoodies, sticking a windmill on his house, going jogging, shafting the LibDems – the list is endless. If you're scraping around in the mud and muck of

British politics like that there's no dignity on offer. Nick Clegg: Nick Clegg. Game over.

But then all you need is Remembrance Sunday, or maybe the centenary of the First World War or the D-Day 70th, when there's the chance to stand still for long periods, stare into the middle distance and try to pull the most noble face you possibly can.

Now, this takes a lot of effort if you're not used to being at all noble. Here's my six-point plan for looking noble when you're not used to looking noble at state occasions:

1. Think sad thoughts. Actors do this sometimes to make themselves cry.* Don't overcook it though and think of the time your dog got run over and weep openly. Crying at the Cenotaph isn't noble, in fact it's quite the opposite: you'll have people somehow saying you disrespect the war dead. Maybe think about when your team went out of the FA Cup in the round you expected them to go out. Sad, but expected.

2. If you wear glasses, take them off, if you wear lenses, take them out. One of the keys to acting noble is to move slightly awkwardly, with stiff, mannered movements. If you can't quite see where

*I don't cry, by the way. It's a strength of mine I'm quite proud of. This is why I could never be an actor.

you're going then you'll deliver that stuff in spades. It also helps with the business of squinting into the middle distance.

3. Squint into the middle distance. This can pass for a noble face if you really can't muster it, for whatever reason: you're hung-over, you did something last night with two prostitutes that you'd been wondering about for years, you're worried about the insurance claim you put in on the Beemer. Focus on a distant fire exit as the 'Last Post' sounds and hope the BBC's cameras get you in shot as you hit maximum noble squinting.

4. Chin up. Chin up is noble.

5. Wear a normal poppy but one with the sprig of green on it. That's as far as you can reasonably pimp your poppy. It seems there are some people who think it's right to honour the war dead by wearing a poppy like a crimson, jewel-encrusted hub-cap. OK, people died for your right to wear a tawdry showy piece of shitty tat like that but don't take the piss.

6. Don't whatever you do wear a donkey jacket. Youngsters reading this wishing to get to grips with the state of the nation might wonder why I say this, but back in the early 80s the Labour Party were led by a mad professor bloke called Michael Foot. The

silly sod turned up at the Cenotaph in an outfit that meant his manifesto in '83 could have promised free booze and bacon sandwiches for life and still no one would have voted for him.

Looking noble is a fine art. And an important one. It's something you need in your political Swiss Army knife. And before you rush to condemn my apparent cynicism here: millions of people died for my right to look noble. So shut it.

Vested interests: take off your vests and fight!

There's too much innuendo in politics these days. Mind you, I'd like to tick Theresa May's box.

Helmut Cleaner, 69, retired fudge packer

THE MEDIA

It's amazing that the amount of news that happens in the world every day always just exactly fits the newspaper. Jerry Seinfeld. I prefer George, though.

I don't want to go all Eric Cantona on you, but you know how a shark has those fish that swim around its nose and feed on the scraps, well if you think about it – and not that hard – the media is the same thing to politics. Well, it used to be before. Politicians were treated with respect, they were allowed not just to finish their sentences but talk in entire paragraphs, no one had even heard of a 'gaffe' and even if anyone had made any they wouldn't have reported it. You could merrily shag who you liked and no one knew nor cared. Churchill was half dead for a big chunk of his second term and no one even knew – his cigars had to be smoked for him by heart/lung machines, in the end. Better times. **Besides, a half-dead Churchill would be better than any of the current crop of pinheads.**

In this day and age it's the other way round: the media is the shark and the politicians are the tiny fish swimming to keep up. If you're one of those people who can be bothered to watch *Newsnight* you can see the grisly spectacle of a politician being sliced and diced and fed to the cat like so much off liver. If your politician actually answers a question they'll pull his answer to pieces, if they don't answer a question they'll have their guts for garters and gaiters and the rest. It's got to the point where it's not so much the media is the tail wagging the dog as the dog is now 98 per cent tail.

If you were an alien who'd crash landed here, before you were put back in a rocket by the UK Border Agency (Space Division), you might be forgiven for thinking that the media were trying to wreck the entire process and drive everyone insane (just because he's crash landed doesn't mean he's an idiot). It's turned into a merry-go-round, a funfair of bullshit – the prize being a goldfish in a bag of water, presented by big-eared ringmaster Andrew Marr.

Examples? Well, the one that sticks like a gallstone halfway down your pee-pipe that isn't anything like as small as the urologist said it would be, is the business of speeches. What happens is this. The Party Leader is scheduled to make a big speech, to the kind of folk who listen to speeches. Yeah, them. So what the Leader's people do to make sure other people get to hear about this speech is they tell the papers or the TV – either by leaking it or far, far worse by giving them a copy of the effing speech – what the Leader is going to say in tomorrow's speech. Well, in that case why not do the speech today, **you complete and utter wank-**

trumpets? The news always used to be what happened yesterday or earlier today, not what is going to be said tomorrow. This totally bonkers mental state of affairs means you end up with similar fuckberks on the radio reacting to the speech BEFORE IT HAS BEEN DELIVERED. Who is this for? What is the point? Do you all want me to hate you?

Political advisers

This whole sorry mess can (in part) be attributed to how much power is wielded by the party political puppet-masters – those silent, sinister backroom press boys who . . . er, lurk in the backrooms.

Take, for instance, Tony Blair's right-hand man, Alastair Campbell. It's common knowledge that he was the biggest super bastard on the block. For instance, he ensured that if someone were to ask Blair an awkward question, such as, 'Prime Minister – can you tell me what the time is, as my watch appears to have stopped?' Campbell would make a 'cut' motion with his hand towards his own neck, and get one of the State's techie henchmen to play 'Things Can Only Get Better' very loudly to drown out the hack. We're through the looking glass, ladies and gentlemen.

Concreting over the political landscape

Live! Outside!

When you watch the news, what do you want to see?
The news. The reporter to tell us what happened,
ideally. Maybe some film of it happening. What we don't
want is a reporter stood outside somewhere, anywhere,
LIVE that is somehow, anyhow, related to what's going
on being asked by another reporter what he or she
reckons might have happened. It makes me want to
fight them, bare-knuckle, shouting 'JUST TELL ME WHAT
HAPPENED AND THEN MOVE ON TO ANOTHER STORY.'
I'm one of life's cowards, trust me, but I'd do time for
this, I can tell you.

Political correspondents

When we switch the TV on, who is it we see outside
Number Ten or on Parliament Square – LIVE? There,
huddled in a raincoat, the BBC's very own **Nick
Robinson** looks into the camera and tells us 'we can
expect this from the government' and 'we can expect
that from the government', without so much as a flicker
from his dead eyes: as welcome as Dennis Skinner at
Nigel Farage's bridge night or a skid mark on an Olympic
gymnast's pearly white leotard. If he's our political eyes
and ears, then it's **Andrew Neil**'s job to provide us with
in-depth, up-to-the-minute analysis and the comedy
timing of a recently deceased guinea pig. As a nation we
can afford to be slightly philosophical about the media's

shambolic political coverage; however, in my opinion the BBC should hang its head in shame at the unceasingly woeful parodies featured on *This Week*, which threaten to make us the laughing stock of Europe (not good laughter – ironic laughter). Quentin Letts, alone, should have his satire licence revoked, and Neil be stripped of all access to hair care products.

Balance

And then there's **balance**. Oh, God help us. Balance will destroy us all. Balance means if you have thirty seconds of one side you have to have thirty seconds of the other. This means even if one side is talking complete and utter total sense, we have to hear from the other side. Who will reply with complete and utter total shit that has to be taken equally seriously. And rather than one of our reporters, who just a moment ago was dead keen

'ASBOs for all'

on sharing his opinion with some plank LIVE from under an umbrella outside who knows where, blowing a hearty raspberry, flicking Vs and saying, '**Well, that was a load of bollocks**,' they keep a straight face. Ask yourself this: **Did the BBC wonder whether Hitler had a point**? The bastards. It is like they want us to hate them.

QUESTION TIME

Chaired by Dame David Dimbleby, the BBC's flagship political and current affairs debating programme has served as a platform for people to voice their opinion and shout at one another for over thirty years. However, there are those who say that it's nothing more than sixty minutes of immature point-scoring interspersed by David Starkey getting his knickers in a twist, Germaine Greer calling out Pol Pot, everyone laughing at something the clever one out of Mitchell & Webb said and George Galloway trying to get Caroline Flint's phone number in the green room afterwards. Like PMQs, it makes you search the house for a claw hammer to smash yourself in the crotch with, just to feel something, anything else.

So, to summarize, it's a nightmare, and for that reason it's brilliant

Because it's such a nightmare, and because everyone knows it – chiefly the people watching it – it means that you don't have to worry about whether you get your message across or not, you can blame the media. Bingo!

✗ Piss-poor policy? No! You've been misrepresented in the media!

- ✗ Party feuding? Don't be daft, it's the media stirring things up!
- ✗ Lose an election because you couldn't organize a piss-up in a brewery? That bastard Murdoch bastard bastard Murdoch! Mainstream Media! MSM! Bastard Murdoch! Murdoch bastard bastard Murdoch! Bastard bastard Murdoch! BBC lefties! BBC Tories! BBC! BBC! Bastards bastards bastards bastards!
- ✗ Your Regional News bastards bastards ITV2 Showbiz News bastards! Bastards!

Boom! See, you're laughing!

You would save money spent lavished on Mickey Mouse media training by going down the pub and hatching paranoid explanations for how you come across. Anyway, you shouldn't worry about media training: it consists of saying 'I'm glad you asked me that question' and then answering another question you've asked yourself. Easy. It must be, Ed Miliband has mastered it. Oh, and before you ask, he's glad you asked him that question. Even better, get on the news the whole time and bang on about how you're not on the news. Why bother getting your message across when you can get that message across and come over as the big fat victim? **Common Sense**. Big fat victim beats an argument every time. Except, of course, when it's Eric Pickles – too much fat, too little argument.

And remember, 'My comments were taken out of context' means 'I was pissed'.

'Drink don't think'

'Forward with movement'

1980S POLITICS: VALLEY OF THE GIANTS, TALES OF YORE

Everyone wants to be immortal. Few are. Margaret Thatcher is. Why? Because her values are timeless, eternal. Tap anyone on the shoulder anywhere in the world, and ask what Mrs Thatcher believed in, and they will tell you. They can give a clear answer to what she 'stood for'.   Maurice Saatchi, pompous berk

No British politician has ever been more despised by the British people than Margaret Thatcher.   Morrissey, miserable git

Politics in the 1980s is something that everyone has an opinion on, even though it's almost properly a long time ago. It could even be classed as history. That has taken some people a lot of getting used to; I for one still find it hard to take the opinions of anyone born after the Falklands War at all seriously and certainly won't have anyone born after 1982 as a boss. Principle. And as time marches on I'm starting to feel the same about people who haven't heard of Operation Desert Storm.

But the 80s was a time of titanic struggle, a battle between good and evil and all that, and there is no way of saying anything about it that won't set off someone. It was all about big clashes, with big changes and big issues, but it's almost too big to talk about and do it justice. Also a lot of it is really boring, if I'm honest. Lot of arguing about Westland Helicopters at one point. Yeah. And the thing is, we will never get the young people of the UK engaged with politics properly unless we explain it in terms they will understand.

'Did Magna Carta die in vain?'
T Hancock

Now even the most out of touch old sod knows that the youth of today when it's not sending pictures of its genitals to each other and taking drugs that you and I haven't heard of (or indeed thought to bother trying: maybe my generation lacked imagination but we would never have tried plant food, let alone called it Meow Meow) is into sci-fi and fantasy stuff. You know, *The Hobbit*, *The Avengers*, *Game of Thrones* – which is as far as I can tell *The Hobbit* for people who can't concentrate unless there's a naked lady every four to five minutes. I love that show. It's like they made it for me, though I don't know the names of any of the characters.

So perhaps the best way to explain it and get the kids to understand the political clashes of the 1980s is as if it all happened three thousand years ago and got written down by some Bronze Age bloke on tablets with a chisel. What you need to make this stuff stick, of course, is lots of middle names beginning with R. Much of the action takes place in Middle England.

The MagWitch

The MagWitch seized power after the longest winter the world has ever known, when the dead were wandering around in bin bags and there was wailing and gnashing of teeth throughout the land. At first, the MagWitch spoke gently, but soon enough she revealed herself prepared to stop at nothing before the country was slain, lame or mewling with pain.

When not eating babies and gargling on the blood of dead Argies, the MagWitch set about dismantling the perfect world created by Clement Attlee and the Pilgrim Fathers of the Labour Party. Before she became PM the MagWitch destroyed the blueprints for milk. Brooding in her lair in Downing Street, with her grog-addled concubine Denis, Torree Partee Grandees would prostrate themselves before the MagWitch in hope of her blessing, but all too many were turned to ash simply because they flew too close to the searing heat of her righteous anger.

Not content with personally punching in the face every single unemployed mineworker (whose P45s she sealed personally with the wax that oozed from her foul teats) and shattering the hopes of young ballet dancers from the North East, she sank the whole Argentinian Armada wearing the hides of a thousand teachers in an utterly unprovoked attack before scorching Scotland repeatedly with nuclear fire. And the Poll Tax: which was so dangerous it caused people to riot spontaneously and vomit blood and piss fire in the street, and turn into bats. In spite of all this she won three elections – no one knows how, impossible to explain.

The Professor, Michael Foot

Michael Foot, a doddering ancient mad professor, returned to earth from the outer reaches of the solar system to do battle with the MagWitch. He had been summoned by the Labour Party because it knew how dangerous the MagWitch was and needed its very best man on the job. Old and frail, and renowned as one of the wisest men in the land, with wild hair and clad in the humble skin of a donkey, he stood no chance against the MagWitch's laser eyes and death-odour, a foul and fetid smell that either killed you or turned you into a loyal zombie supporter.

Unably assisted by the likes of Denis Healey, whose only form of protection was a shield made of huge eyebrows consisting of long poison-tipped quills, and the clinically dissident Wedgwood Benn, a man incapable of agreeing even with himself, Mad Michael blew it completely. His chief problem was he kept coming up with mad hare-brained ideas like selling off the Queen and knighting all teachers, as well as paying the dwarfish coalminers in the gold talents the MagWitch had been hoarding beneath her Palace in Westminster. The MagWitch laughed in the face of Professor Foot, scoffed at his uncosted dreams and destroyed him and his hopes in the 1983 election, the result of which no one can explain by any rational means, given how evil she was.

The Ki'Nnock

And so it came to pass that the MagWitch could not be defeated. And a call came out from the deepest void in the ancient bowels of the Welsh Mountains, and a ruddy Celtic Warrior heeded this call: and his name was the Ki'Nnock. Comb-over blazing like righteous red fire, the Ki'Nnock marched forward, wading through the deepest mists of policy, smiting enemies and allies alike, and in overlong sentences that never quite landed his point, did noble battle with the MagWitch. The Ki'Nnock warned the world not to grow old, not to want to go to college, but even his magical words and incantations could not halt the progress of time. The MagWitch also called to her side the creature from the DownUnderworld, Rupert Morlock, who beamed the powerful rays of the *Sun* directly into the Ki'Nnock's eyes. The Ki'Nnock's spells and sentences were too long and the *Sun* boiled them down to tiny, meaningless fragments. Shattered, defeated and destroyed, the Ki'Nnock crawled across the sea to a new home in the belly of Brussels, where his wounds were soothed and his efforts eased away with balm and nice car and expense account.

Following the Ki'Nnock came the Honest Smith – cruelly taken before his time – then the Devil-Eyed Blair-Worm – he would stare at you so powerfully you believed everything he said, but by then the MagWitch had perished, her deeds undone, her plans for strangling everyone in the entire country with her bare hands, and bathing the North in hot fire, thwarted because she failed to win by the necessary 15 per cent margin of the votes cast of 372 MPs in the Conservative Party leadership contest against Michael Heseltine in early November of 1990, though the Tories went on to win the general election in 1992 under John Major.

I'd go on but HBO are on the phone, they want to adapt this as soon as possible once I've written some norks into it.

LAND OF CONFUSION

Tell me why this is the land of confusion, oh-oh-oh.
Genesis, 'Land of Confusion'

The modern world is a confusing place. No one would argue with that. Sometimes you don't know which way to turn, sometimes it seems like just getting a straight answer out of someone is as hard as waiting in for a parcel to be delivered.*

Take job titles. Job titles used to be simple, plain, straightforward. Take, for instance, these four jobs. Manager. Builder. Clerk. Train driver. Not any more. Systems Development Co-ordination Management Assistant. That could be any of those four jobs these days.

So one thing we could all do for ourselves is make things simpler.

*WHY IS THAT SO BLOODY DIFFICULT?? WHAT IS WRONG WITH THESE PEOPLE???

'Forwards into the past!'

Admit it, you'd like that, wouldn't you? Life is complicated, complex, hard to get to grips with, brushing out some of the confusion and helping us all to be that little bit more easy to understand would go a long way.

Well here's what we should do. Clear up one of the most confusing things at the heart of how people go about their daily lives – especially bar staff I can tell you: the confusion between the words **couple**, **few** and **several**.

People insist on using these words all the time, when they could manage perfectly well with numbers. Numbers offer you the chance to be precise, to actually specify how many drinks you had, for instance.

The alternative, alternative

Words, on the other hand, do not help with this process. Not one bit. Now, two pints would be two pints, wouldn't it, yet very often I see men saying they've had a couple of pints when they've had no such thing. Unless their idea of a **loving couple** is a **nine-man, two-woman gang bang**.*

So: a firm definition of what constitutes a couple is this, even in these morally lax times – it means two. A couple = two.

But let's go back. I'll count for you now using words rather than numbers: one couple, few, several, many, lots, plenty. Now these words sound like they offer loads of grey areas but truth be told they are highly accurate, reliable words that have strict and accurate numerical meanings, and they are as follows. Or at least they ought to be, and if I had my way they would be, enforceable with local byelaws.

*Stop thinking about that, I'm trying to make a point here, Squire.

'One' is one

And all alone and ever more shall be so. And the Queen.

'A couple' is two

Everyone knows that. Two people in a couple. A couple of eggs with your bacon, everyone understands what a couple is. So when you want to say two, you can say couple and the job is done.

'A few': well that's three

A few is more than a couple, obviously, but a few is nowhere near as many as four. So it can only really be three – if you have a few of something you have three of them. Stands to reason. And anyone who has ever struggled with maths and numbers and stuff will know that none of it stands to reason, so to find something numerical that does is quite a breakthrough. So a few is three. No more no less.

Which brings us to 'several'

Several is nothing too complicated, it shouldn't cause confusion, but it seems that often enough people do get confused because it has the sound of seven in it, it is in fact nothing to do with seven, never has been, never will be.

Rules is rules - pint for the fella, you know the rest.

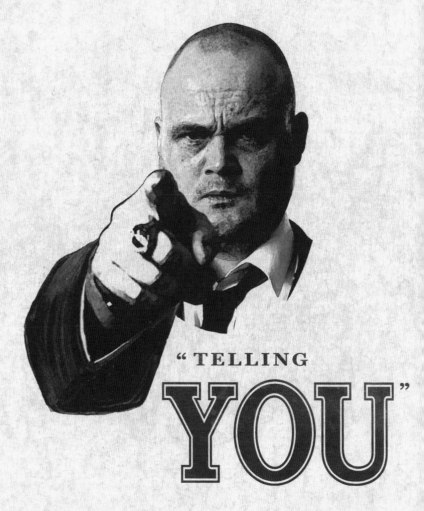

BRITONS

"TELLING

YOU"

WHAT YOU WANT TO HEAR

GOD SAVE THE FUKP PARTY

Wear hi-viz for reasons of gravitas.

Baby kissing: never practise on a real baby.

Patriotism - sexy. Deny it.

CHEZ LANDLORD

FUKP is not a spacist party.

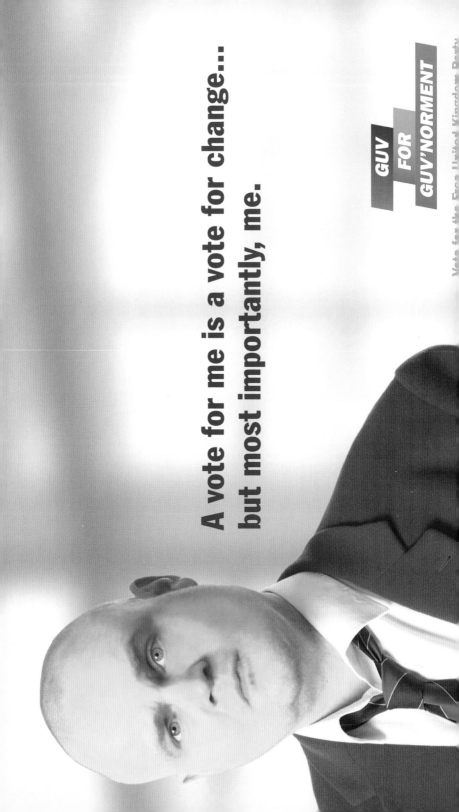

It is not even a cousin of seven, never has been, never will be.

But several, by a process of logical deduction can only really be one thing, and that is four. If you've got a couple doing two – which is its job no argument – a few doing three – what else could it do? – then that leaves the door wide open to several having to be four, and, frankly, what else could it be?

After that you've got **many**, which is **five**, **lots**, which is **six**, and **plenty**, which is **seven**. And I think if you apply this in a **Common Sense** manner to an evening's drinking you'll agree with me that I'm right, and that the country would benefit from a standardization of the language. We've had governments faffing around with all sorts of nonsense over the last few years and not one of them has sought to bring this whole area of utter confusion under control.

A vote for me is a vote for change... but most importantly, me.

GREAT BRITONS

NO. 47: RICHARD BRANSON

Britain can be proud of its almost unparalleled ability to produce Great Britons. From Isambard Kingdom Brunel to David Seaman, from General Montgomery to Penelope Keith, from Shakespeare to Len Goodman we keep churning out these amazing individuals who leave their indelible mark on history, which can't be removed.

Some men are born to follow. Some men are born to lead – and some men are born to make it possible for Mike Oldfield to compose a cover version of the *Blue Peter* theme while sat cross-legged. Of course, I'm talking about yet another one of Britain's finest – Sir Richard Branson: entrepreneur; adventurer; and of course the man who charges you four quid to use Wi-Fi on his trains. But I digress.

From exhaustive research, what becomes abundantly clear from looking at his Wikipedia page are three things: firstly, at the age of sixty-four, Branson is one of Britain's richest sixty-four-year-old men; secondly, there's nothing here about the availability of free drinks on his space shuttle; and finally, they could've used a better picture than that one.

A major problem Sir Richard faced in his formative days as an entrepreneur was that he was forced to change his name from 'Branston' to 'Branson'. This was because people would regularly confuse him with Branston Shopfitters, a well-known company that was based in Carlisle. This steely determination was enough to show the business community that here was a man who wasn't going to let living in a really nice house with kind, supportive parents and having some nice chums deter him from one day sailing across the Atlantic Ocean in a hot-air balloon and owning a finance company that could offer its customers fixed-rate ISAs.

One of Branson's colleagues said that his go-getting, problem-solving attitude is legendary: 'Richard's, like, totally awesome. I remember this one time when we were in a restaurant – I'd ordered fish, and he'd ordered steak. The problem was, the waiter made a mistake and gave us the wrong meals! So quick as a flash Richard took it upon himself to swap the two plates around so I had the food I'd ordered and he had the food he'd ordered, thus averting a horrendous wrong-meal scenario. Come to think of it now, a negative, glass half-empty person who's probably on benefits or something, would've eaten the meal they didn't want, whereas Richard sat in his chair and did something about it. That's the measure of the man.'

Poverty is just a word invented by plebs to make us feel bad about making loads of money. Or indeed inheriting it.

Duchess Daisy of Hazzard, 61, First Lady of Boss-Hogg House

MEN OF THE MOMENT: NIGEL FARAGE

Well, there's no denying that this man is the electric eel of British politics. He's given the whole thing a great big shock, he's great on TV, he comes across as reasonable and everything. He's done what they call 'galvanized' things, though quite how he's prevented politics from rusting in damp conditions by the method of electrolytic conversion will have to remain unexplained.

He's even sometimes talked about using **Common Sense**, though I would beg to differ.

And all the while, there he is,

hiding in plain sight.

That's it, you see. Nigel Farage is, without doubt, a sleeper agent. WAKE UP SHEEPLE! You need evidence? It's staring you in the face. Right there in front of you. Obvious. But oh so clever. If it wasn't something you saw every day it'd be the first thing you noticed. **Look at his name! It's French!**

Once you realize this it's clear that this is the only rational explanation for how he's been carrying on. Join up the dots. It's there to be seen. Open your eyes. Ask yourself this: who is he really?

That's right. **Family tells you everything.** Everything you need to know. Farage's family was sent over amongst Huguenot refugees seeking asylum in England as hidden long-term sleeper agents in the 1700s. French foreign policy has long maintained that a weakened UK is good for France. In the old days that went so far as France forming an alliance with the Scots. The French then ditched the Scots the minute they didn't think they were any use to them; that's the measure of the people we are dealing with here. One French Foreign Minister called Vergennes once said: 'It is more possible that a good Christian should form an alliance with the devil than I with England.' See?

But enough **Big Picture logical deduction**. What is clear is this: some time in the mid-1990s Farage was activated, and the seeds of chaos were sown.

Attaching himself to the anti-European party UKIP was his masterstroke, and a true sign of the deep-down Gallic deviousness at his plan's heart. No one would expect a Euro stooge, sent by François Mitterrand and Jacques Delors via sealed orders from Cardinal Richelieu cc'd to Napoleon himself, to wreak chaos. UKIP was a fringe party for the people John Major had pissed off

– on reflection it's surprising it wasn't a bigger party at the start.

The cover story is almost perfect. Yes he went to private school like all those other people who went to private school, so he's been trained, from childhood, in how those people think. But then he didn't go to Oxbridge, precisely so he could create a cover story as someone not from the Establishment. Very, very clever. In fact I'd go so far as to say brilliant. Worthy of Marshal Pétain, the hero of Verdun, whose mastery of the long game was unmatched.

Then he went into business. Admittedly, becoming a metals trader in the City wasn't the outsider role he was perhaps looking for, but Huguenot training required him to fuel up on tons of money to be able to then create mayhem in the UK. This kind of forward planning is a lesson bitterly learned by France's investment in the Maginot Line; tactical flexibility is paramount.

You've got to admit it's quite brilliant. No one would ever suspect this, but a simple glance at Wikipedia and you can divine his actual motives, his innermost thoughts. It's all there. You couldn't make it up. **He can deny it all you like, but then he's been trained to deny it. That proves who he really is. Cast-iron, copper-bottomed proof.**

'Come on, he's never been heard to speak French,' you might reply. Exactly. See? See how it works? The word 'coup' is French. It's all there.

He got elected as an MEP. Perfect. Well, I say elected. No one votes in European elections, so it wasn't the public turning out for him, it was the Gallic Underground. His seat in the Euro Parliament means he can come and go from Europe without attracting attention. Not too often, mind, so as not to blow his cover. After all, he says he doesn't like the place and what it stands for so why would he bother turning up? That's principle in action right there. Or looks like it! And it is full of Germans and Frenchies and Italians and Belgians and whoever else is in the Common Market, so you can hardly blame him, say his advocates. It's the perfect cover.

The more he does what he can to destabilize the UK the happier the French are, and the Germans, who sent his German wife to the UK to work closely with him. He casts himself as the friend of ordinary British people, yet every night, I expect, he goes into his loft, and with the radio set smuggled to the UK from Strasbourg piece by piece **up his bumhole**, probably, reports back to the Direction Générale de la Sécurité Extérieure. Dee dit dit dee dee dee, dee dit dit dee dee dee. All night long.

And they're all at it. Look: France is being run by a Dutch bloke, Hollande. Russia's President is a man with a surname that almost means prostitute in French. And Germany by a woman. Classic French move. Hiding in plain sight.

'But how can we be sure, Guv?' you ask. 'How can we possibly know this is right?' Well, all you have to do is think about it. Think of it like when you squint really hard at a picture and you can see a pair of tits in it. Or those pictures of criminals with their faces pixelated out: rub your eyes and you can make out what they look like. **All he has to do is say something about Europe and how much he doesn't like it and he shores up his cover. Genius.** And in the meantime, the UK is riven by division and can't get down to its usual political business of the Labour and Tory parties calling each other names.

Politics is like, hummus on a gorilla's head with like, David Miliband riding a pink wafer through a den of squirrels with boners. Random.

Nathaniel Flopdoodle, 23, surrealist comedian (real name Gary Stevens)

DEMOCRACY

Democracy is the process by which people choose the man who'll get the blame.   Bertrand Russell

One thing that is worth remembering is that this country isn't a democracy.

It's a version of one, but not a true democracy.

A true democracy is what?

A true democracy is when all points of view are considered, all conditions weighed up, all positions honoured, everyone gets what they want. In other words, it's **like trying to leave the house on a Sunday morning with two teenaged daughters**. The central heating is blazing, there's no hot water left and you're three and a half hours late for lunch.

Compromise – it's a promise neither of you wants to keep

Actually how you make decisions about the central heating is a good way of looking at the business of compromise.

28 degrees

We could all leave the heating on all day at 28 degrees. Is that Centigrade? Another example of Brussels worming its way into our lives. Sure your gas bill would be enormous, but you'd be able to save on laundry by wandering around in the buff. So your electricity bill would be a lot smaller. And your spending on Ariel. But you'd still need clothes, for when you went out and for when you answered the door. No one wants to answer the door in the nude; life isn't a porn film (more's the pity). So there'd be the business of getting dressed whenever the doorbell went. And the house being really hot, though no one wants to admit it, can cause tempers to fray; arguments would follow. You have to think these things through.

24 degrees

So obviously having your heating at that absurd heat won't work. You'll need to knock it down a few degrees. So you do and as a result you can walk around the house in a T-shirt. It's what: 24 degrees. It's still really warm, any kind of exertion – DIY, reaching for the remote more than once, a hefty crap – makes you sweat. Your heating bill is still really big AND you aren't feeling the saving benefit of not having to do any laundry. On the other hand, tempers would not be as much affected; you'd have to envisage fewer rows.

22 degrees

So you knock it down a couple of degrees to 22. Some-one find out what that is in Fahrenheit. On a really cold day the heating might struggle to keep up, but this is a much more realistic temperature for the smooth running of a household. And you're saving money: you're doing laundry but you can dry the clothes on your radiators. Smooth moves. Win–win. Give yourself a biscuit.

Thing is, you get to 22 degrees and you might as well drop it down to 20. Why not? Put on an extra jumper, make yourself a nice warm cuppa. And then sneak the thermostat down to 18 degrees. Bosh. Gas is off, no more gas bill. OK you can't dry your clothes on the rads, but it'll be cold enough that you'll never break a sweat and you'll be able to wear your clothes until they fall apart.

Now this is all a practical and rational way of looking at the business of your central heating. But what it fails to take into account is the fact that one or maybe more people in this arrangement might be a woman and they will, whatever you set the heating at, turn it up. No matter how you might have carefully weighed up what you want to do with the central heating you will have to compromise. Even though you were compromising with actual reality itself.

So look forward to arguing in a sweat-soaked fleece in a house so hot the air makes you cry hot salt tears and shrivels your tonsils to gristle and your thoughts turn bitterly to divorce.

At the heart of every democratic decision is this very issue: the clash between reality as it stands and then what people think they want.

Which is why you get people moaning about how it doesn't work because they haven't got what they want right now. Like fucking toddlers. Who would think up such a terrible way of doing things? Well, you know who's been in the news lately, causing a commotion? The Greeks, that's who.

The Greeks invented it: don't let that put you off

That's right, the Greeks invented democracy. Along with other stuff, like philosophy, astronomy, the kebab and that fella-on-fella business. Four out of five ain't bad. I don't want to marry a man. It's surprising really how much the Greeks achieved, it's up there with the fact that the Romans were Italian.

Democracy was invented in Athens, where they'd been through all sorts of dramas. Not those long boring plays about incest they were into back then, but wars with other Greeks, wars with Persians, wars with whoever else they could get their hands on. They did a lot of this fighting in sandals, I expect – not too sure, to be honest. Fighting in sandals would give anyone fighting in steel-toecapped DMs an immediate and unfair advantage.

Most of the people who lived in Athens were slaves, but please don't let that get in the way of your enjoyment of this nice story about the birth of freedom. Your Athenian would vote on everything, however: there were no proper laws as such and that meant they were making it up as they went along. So when a decision came up they'd vote on it; very direct: sounds good.

I can see a lot of benefits to that but also plenty of problems with it. All it would take is some smooth talker to stir things up and the next thing you know **you'd be off having a war in Persia or somewhere just because some crazy goggle-eyed sod spun you a line**. Imagine that. Doesn't bear thinking about. **Wouldn't happen here.**

So the Greeks set the ball rolling. Government of the people by the people for the people. It sounds peachy, doesn't it?

Actually, I know a fair few people – I expect you do too – and the problems are these:

✗ They don't give a shit about much particularly.

✘ They can't be bothered about anyone else.

✘ Their default setting is bone-idle.

These three eternal human qualities would seem to be **democratic Kryptonite**. Add to that the fact that none of them seem to be able to organize something as simple as car insurance and it's obvious they're probably not going to be interested in governing either the people, or by the people, or for the people. Well, I know they're not. And thank God for that. The idea of **Irish Geoff** having anything to do with how the country is run is utterly terrifying. You don't want him involved, let me tell you that much. Unflushed toilets on a national scale? Disputes settled with broken little fingers? No one should have to live like that.

But the point is, I think it's a given that none of us really wants to run the country; it looks like a lot of hassle, hard work. In fact it could be, what with the way things are in modern politics, that, like Spurs winning the Premiership, effective government is simply impossible in the modern era, so why would we bother trying? When there's a bunch of tossers willing to do it for us.

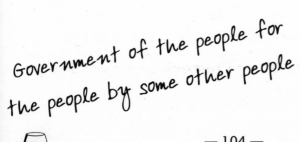

Government of the people for the people by some other people

PARLIAMENT: *n.*
TALKING SHOP

Parliament, which is our Beautiful British version of democracy, first appeared 750 years ago in these fair isles of ours, and I will have to admit that it was a French bloke called **Simon de Montfort** whose idea it was. He was fed up with the way things were going in England – even though, being French, I can't imagine what business it was of his, the bastard – and ordered the King to meet him for a conference with the other top knobs of the day.

Now: you'll notice this wasn't by the people for the people. It was by the knobs for the knobs, of the King, so we've come a long way in 750 years. The House of Lords ran the House of Commons, it was a way of getting everyone together at once so they could explain slowly and simply to the King that they hated paying taxes. They were only human.

Basically, that became Parliament's job for about another 400 years. They hated paying taxes because, well, **everyone hates paying taxes**.

But it wasn't until **Oliver Cromwell** came along that Parliament started to matter.

Magnerer Carterer

King Charles I hadn't called Parliament for ages and that suited everyone. Eleven years. Eleven sweet years. Imagine that. No one liked being called into London so they could be told they had to go home again and take monies off people – it upset the apple cart. As it happens, this sounds ideal, doesn't it? No tedious elections, no one collecting taxes, the knobs and royals keeping themselves to themselves. Were we ever so free?

Then the King ran out of money – and he called Parliament. Parliament wasn't happy (this was before expense accounts had been invented), so once it had turned up, it made life difficult for the King. And fair enough. You'd not want to have to stop whatever you were doing and come into London to pay your taxes. So this time Parliament tried to get the King under control and . . . well look, you don't need to know all this but the upshot was **Oliver Cromwell chopped the King's head off and then banned Christmas**. If you want to piss off the British public then that's it right there, as a one–two, the original double-whammy.

A new King came back but Parliament stayed. And that's pretty much where we've been ever since, with the King or Queen gradually having less to do and less power and Parliament becoming more and more important, with Prime Ministers and all that coming along as it went. God help us.

HOW DOES PARLIAMENT WORK?

The English think they are free. They are free only during the election of members of Parliament.
Jean-Jacques Rousseau

Yeah, well, beats being French and in the Stranglers, pal. Jog on.

A lot like the railways

Right.

Parliament in its current form is a lot like the railways.

Perfected under the Victorians, the envy of the world, exported to grateful eager nations. Magnificent buildings, temples to democracy, the new cathedrals of progress. Houses of Parliament: St Pancras station. Spot the difference.

Well the difference is the railways have been updated since. Steam is long gone. Most lines have been electrified. There's even Wi-Fi in some carriages as long as the train is going past a hill, or a field or maybe it's overcast. (The state of Wi-Fi on trains isn't helping me make my point here, so I'll move on.)

But Parliament hasn't had the refit it should have, and the building and its institutions have been crumbling ever since. Parliament still has the old signals, the same points, some of the same old rolling stock. Every time you go into a shiny new railway station like that nice station at King's Cross or Newcastle or Manchester Piccadilly that's what Parliament ought to be like but ain't. Modern loos, proper refreshments, ticket machines that take visa cards. Now: I like the past as much as anyone sensible, and know for a fact I'd much rather have had thirty short smallpox-riddled years as a Georgian or Victorian as the world trembled at the merest mention of the Royal Navy than eighty-five years in this scaredy-cat drone-fighting political-correctness-gone-mad era – but the simple fact is the railways have had a refit and they can only just cope. Parliament hasn't and looks like it can't.

Enough metaphor bollocks, Guv, what are the basics?

Rubbing politics' nose in its own mess

It works like this.

- ✗ MPs are elected at general elections, or by-elections.
- ✗ There are general elections every five years except when they're every four years or whenever there has to be one.
- ✗ 650 MPs represent the people who voted for them in their constituency *and* the people who didn't vote for them *and* their own party.*
- ✗ One side is the government the other side is the opposition, but both sides are a total shower of shit: there, I said it.
- ✗ There's a fella called Mr Speaker and MPs say everything to him for some reason, probably that they can't even look each other in the eye what with the bollocks they're coming out with.
- ✗ There's a thing called Prime Minister's Questions – PMQs if you're into that stuff – a spectacle that is so terrible it makes you want to pick up a claw hammer and smash off your own penis just to experience something better.
- ✗ The House of Lords is full of people you might be forgiven for thinking were dead and/or in prison.*
- ✗ The Queen turns up and opens it once a year and has to read out a speech which says what her

*Yes this is right.
*And some of whom are.

government is going to do. She does this without once sounding sarcastic, God bless her, she's the best of the lot: she's a marvel; she drove a lorry in the war don't you know.

✗ All the MPs are doing when they're not shouting is filling in expenses claims for cough sweets from getting sore throats from shouting.

✗ Ladies who are MPs must surely spend every waking moment thinking: 'Why in God's name am I doing this?'

✗ The clock isn't called Big Ben; that's the name of the bell.

✗ There's a bloke called Black Rod who bangs on the door sometimes; no one really knows why.

✗ The distance between the two sides is the length of two swords, and not only that, there is a room for them to hang their swords up in.

You can if you want try to understand how the whole thing works, the intricacies of government whips and all that, but it's pretty simple really. The government put legislation through the House of Commons and they can do this because they have a majority. Putting stuff through the House of Commons involves all those horrible wanker MPs shouting at each other and then voting. Then the House of Lords talks about it very slowly, sends it back down and the Commons all shout at each other about it again. The Bill gets through. The government wins. Or not. When it doesn't it's really embarrassing for the government and the sort of people who care about this stuff faff on about it.

Honestly, that's it. And somehow that is the most important place in the country. That's how it works, but what does it do, **apart from keeping Keith Vaz off the streets?**

'Throwing a spanner in the political apparatus'

What time is change?

WHAT DOES PARLIAMENT DO?

Well now there's the question that needs answering.

It's the question that springs to the lips of every man, woman and concerned child (probably with leftie parents, the sort of kids who at Christmas parties for five-year-olds say to Santa that they want to be Palestinian for Christmas) every time they see the Palace of Westminster on the telly.

What does Parliament do? Actually? Surely the machinery of modern government is so enormous and faceless, and actually in the hands of countless nameless civil servants, that even the red-faced yelping pillocks on the back benches might only have a dim idea of how the thing really works. Stands to reason. Maybe that's why MPs come across as such a miserable bunch, they've gone through all that slog to get into Parliament and then they've realized they've been sold a pup. I imagine sixteen years on the back benches without so much as a whiff of a government post is as firm a waste of time as anything else, and I'm including supporting Spurs in that.

But the question should be asked. The Lords, the Commons, the select committees, working parties, cross-party commissions, royal inquiries, early day motions, guillotine motions, division lobbies, points of order, the whips' offices,  the secretaries, the under-secretaries, the special advisers, the Strangers Bar, Black Rod, the Speaker, the Serjeant-at-Arms, privy counsellors, Hansard. What does it all do?

Well, what does it all do? Do you know? The thing is, I *don't* know, and I'm actually happy to say that I don't know. And in fact I'd encourage you not to know too. Not because ignorance is bliss, but because it's **the very least** you and I can do. If our politicians are going to give us the finger, the least we can do is flick a firm pair of Vs back.

It's only fair. Go on, fault that logic.

After all: the people in it are completely out of touch with you and me, how we live our lives, what we do, what we think, how the simple daily business of going about our daily business goes, aren't they? So the very least we can do is return the favour and be totally out of touch with them and whatever it is they get up to.

Fault that logic at your peril, Squire.

But wait, there's more

Well, actually I think I will. That attitude, which makes perfect sense without a doubt, isn't good enough, is it? Maybe we could do a bit more than the very least. Truth is, the government – which is run from Parliament – is immensely powerful. In 2014 the government spent **£732 billion**. That's a lot of folding. The fact that in 2014 they only collected **£648 billion** makes that amount of money all the more eye-watering. You wouldn't stay in business long if you ran a hot-dog stand like that. Aside from the fact that you'd need an almost endless supply of hot dogs, you'd probably not make the rent on the stand. It's almost half of the money the UK turns over in a year.

So whether you like it or not what goes on in the House of Commons could be regarded as pretty important. Which is probably why they dress it up like some sort of pantomime. If you were spending **£732 billion** knowing perfectly well you were **£84 billion** in the red you might shout and yell like you'd lost your mind and wave your order papers and boo and make animal noises in a demented manner. It might be the only rational option when you're that much in hock.

You might even hope the public weren't paying attention. You might also get better people on the job but let's not get on to the subject of Ed Miliband right now. It makes me maudlin, it's like Labour doesn't want to win. Put up a fight, you useless bastards.

How does Parliament spend this money? Well, Parliament makes laws. The laws are either 'don't punch that man in the face no matter how annoying he's being', 'don't park your car there, mate' type of laws, or 'we want to read your emails while you're on the toilet for reasons of national security' stuff, or they're the sort of laws that allocate and determine government spending. A lot like one of those business plans you have to submit to your bank manager, which made perfect sense last night on the back of an envelope with Alan's help – and Alan was always good at figures, no doubt about that – but which in the cold light of day don't quite add up.

MPs argue over this stuff, get up and make a speech, reply, someone else butts in and so on, but what it's all about is money. Spending money. Which if it's not the money they've collected it's the money they've borrowed which we then have to pay back.

Which brings me to another point. Imagine being able to get a line of credit that runs to £84 billion. I don't know about you, but that's a fair few quid, isn't it? Then by Jimmy Greaves's beard and all that's holy, count me in.

So you could do a lot worse than pay attention.
Otherwise these wankers will get away with murder.

'Enough of the joke candidates'

'Going to any lengths to fight extremism'

MPS' EXPENSES – WHAT'S ACCEPTABLE?

BANG OUT OF ORDER	ACCEPTABLE
Luxury penthouse suite in Mayfair	Travel Lodge (Croydon South)
Membership of the Garrick Club	Morrisons loyalty card
Chauffer-driven Daimler	Public transport/ABC Minicabs
Michelin-star restaurants	Kansas Fried Chicken
Swimming pool	Swingball
Duckpond	Fishbowl
Grace & favour	Do me a favour
First-class transatlantic flight	Budget long-haul DVT economy
Stationery	Beer mats/Little blue biros from the bookies

Because it's a Marathon, not a Snickers

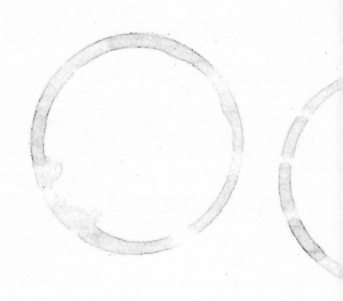

GOVERNMENT: WHAT IS IT FOR?

Whoever wins the election, the government gets in.
That bloke in the pub whose glasses you'd like to stuff up his arse

What is government for? What does it do? Why does it do it?

How often do people ask themselves this?

Not often enough, I'd wager. They just crack on with blaming the government, which is every British man and woman's right under Magna Carta,* just under the bit about fishing rights on the Thames, and rightly so.

But I thought for once I should try to answer this question. According to a quick straw poll in the lounge last Thursday this is what government currently does:

✗ the bins;
✗ the roads;

*Actually, probably not woman's. Magna Carta is pretty light on what rights the ladies have.

- ✗ bans smoking in pubs;
- ✗ benefits;
- ✗ tells me not to eat chips.

Of course, there's lots else besides, but these are the things foremost in people's minds. But notice, none of them mentioned pensions, health, foreign policy or any of that. And why not? Because we conducted the poll in the pub on the day when bin day would have been if the council hadn't bloody gone fortnightly.

But let's break down these functions of government.

What government does: the bins

Why does the government put the bins out? Why don't we do it?

After all, everyone likes a trip to the tip of a Sunday. What could be finer than putting the seats down in the car and filling it up with the stuff that you've been storing up for this special occasion?

The anticipation as you wait in the queue at the tip and wonder to yourself why there are quite so many signs warning you about prosecution if you attack the staff. And then there's the satisfaction of backing your motor into a space by a skip without scraping it on a bollard or another skip.

Lobbing those bin bags into the skips, that's a laugh, looking at what other people have thrown away, imagining their lives for a minute or two and then the brief bit of loitering with intent to do some skip-dipping by the electricals bin to round the whole thing off.

It's a perfect Sunday morning's entertainment, maybe a sneaky Maccy D's on the way there or back, depending on when you're going to have your Sunday roast. So why oh why does the government insist on doing it themselves? It's fun, it gets you out of the house and it's got to be a big chunk of your council tax bill.

So: why does the government do the bins? Well, here the Second Rule of **Common Sense** comes into play: Thinking it Through.

The reason you don't do the bins yourself and that the government does is because clever people in government positions have thought it through for you. They don't want to ruin the joy of going to the tip and to do that, they stop you from going to the tip. That's right. And they do it for your own good and for the good of the country too. Use your imagination, they have.

Imagine the queue if everyone went to the tip every Sunday morning. There'd be you and everyone else you've ever met, lined up on the road by the tip, causing a mile-long tailback, and it would go on all day.

The drive-through at Maccy D's would be gridlocked. And the simple pleasure of clearing out those old mags and slices of carpet you kept just in case and the hedge trimmings and lobbing them into the different coloured skips would be lost.

And that's why the government does the bins, not for reasons of hygiene, mass transit issues, or even control. It does the bins because deep down this is a Christian country – yes, yes it is actually* – and it is doing what it can to keep Sundays special.

This is why we have a government, and this is why the bins is the first thing on the list when you ask people.

What government does: the roads

OK, so if the bins are the last vestige of this country's Christian heritage – and yes they are, and yes this country is a Christian country, don't let anyone tell you otherwise – then what are the roads? Why does the government get to do roads?

The answer is the Romans, of course.

*Just about though not for long hang on in there we have to stand our ground and stand up for Christian values and if that means not loving my neighbours and not turning the other cheek for the time being then so be it.

Roman roads – and they were just straight, went straight everywhere – were the first bits of what you might call government infrastructure spending in the UK. And for better or worse, the Romans went down in history as being the first people to have proper government kind of like you and I might recognize it, what with building roads and the like (I don't know if they put the bins out, I doubt it, archaeologists rely too heavily on the rubbish out the back of people's houses to make that likely).

The Romans brought in laws, language, coinage and the other government stuff. But it's roads that got left behind after they left, after it all went tits up in the fifth century. Basically they took on the British, who didn't like being governed, and after 400 years or so threw in the towel. Bit off more than they could chew.

But what they did was put roads on the map, so to speak. And we British we love our roads, we love driving, we love cars, millions of us go out every day and sit in enormous traffic jams because we just can't get enough of roads. Formula 1, we love talking about cars, we love watching *Top Gear*. We might not have been able to make cars with any degree of efficiency or skill, but that's not the point. We love cars because we love roads.

So any government that wants to make sure the British public are happy and feel like they're being

'Putting the meat on the political promise bones'

properly looked after has to keep the roads going, build more roads, never mind if rail is more efficient or better for the environment or any of that bollocks, what matters is we love roads. End of.

If government tried to get rid of the roads like the Greens want there'd be anarchy. Not only would people be furious at the loss of their God-given right to get about unfettered by timetable (traffic permitting), to go for a potter on a Sunday morning, to burn off your mates at the lights by the bus station, to pick up your nan and bring her over when her boiler breaks down, but the UK would degenerate into a prolonged episode of *Top Gear*, off-roading in a Robin Reliant with hilarious consequences. **Is that the country you want to live in?**

And that's why governments have to do roads, and why as freeborn people of these islands we expect that from government.

PLEASE NOTE: Toll roads we do not like until you get on the M6 toll and put your foot down, stone me that's the way to go, no bastard on it and off you go.

What government does: bans smoking in pubs

Right. Now. This is the thing.

Believe me, civil wars have been started over less. The Civil War in this country was started pretty much over how much reach the King and his mates – an archbishop, apparently – had into people's daily lives. The King wanted to check up on what people believed, what they said and did in church. Now, let's be frank, you could shrug a lot of that off, couldn't you? How many of you go to church anyway? Not as many of you as go to the pub, I'll bet. Nevertheless this kicked off a Civil War and Oliver Cromwell and all that King beheading stuff.

And so Tony Blair, **not content** with **smashing up Afghanistan** and **destroying Iraq** (though I can't knock it, that's **two wins** at the start of the century, though I am disappointed he didn't get a world war in before the millennium and get us the hat-trick on the century) then set about destroying the beautiful British boozer. Thanks a lot, mate.

And why did he do that? Because he was an ex-smoker, that's why. And they're the fucking worst. Smokers – well live the life you want to live, mate, life is nasty brutish and short; make your own decisions. People who've never smoked, that's the path you have chosen, so be it. It's those bastards who've given up and want the rest of the world to know it and suffer like them. Tony Blair has many faults, he did a great deal you can't agree with, and maybe you're one of those people who bangs on about corporations because it makes you think you have an opinion and you could even be one of those people who still calls him Bliar, but here's the thing, the worst, most permanently damaging thing interfering in people's lives he ever did was ban smoking in pubs.

And yes they're much more pleasant to be in now. What there are of them left. Smokers were the lungs of British pubs and they've been suffocated, and British pubs with them. It's almost as though Tony Blair couldn't bear the thought of going somewhere where people enjoyed themselves more than he ever could with his barren joyless life playing that stupid fucking red Stratocaster of his and so set about destroying it. And don't forget his right-hand man Mr Campbell is a reformed alcoholic. Would he cry over closed pubs? Nah.

One day in the future in Sharia Britain (could happen) the imams will stand in their mosque pulpits and will tell stories of how there were places men and some women could go and drink, and that drinking was commonplace, loved by the people, that young women would lie down in the gutter for the love of drink. And the Ayatollah of Canterbury will relate how these places died out, how rather than the Righteous persuading the Kuffar that drink was the very devil, nor because people realized they really didn't like drinking, that it left them unfulfilled and led them somehow through disaffection to the Koran, but **because some boggle-eyed creep and his hand-wringing Ninny State mates knew best**, and drove the drinking places into the ground. Verily Allah moves in a mysterious way, they will say, and light up a fag.

Which brings me to what the ban on smoking in pubs actually is: it's the dying embers of the Civil War itself. And the Roundheads won. Well, count me in as one of the Cavaliers, please, folks.

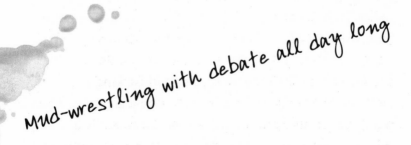

Mud-wrestling with debate all day long

What government does: benefits

Right. Here it is. Benefits. Well, benefits, handouts, the dole, free money, whatever you want to call it. We can meander our way through bins, roads and smoking bans as remnants of Christianity, the Romans and the Civil War but in the end what we have here is an example of government in the modern era.

Benefits are a whole graveyard's worth of contention. No point going on about it. That family with nineteen kids. What the hell is going on there? Those aren't children, they're a benefits-based pyramid scheme. But also that has to be a living hell. One kid is enough to drive you insane from sleep deprivation, two even more. But nineteen? If you're managing nineteen kids and still having more babies, the truth is you're clearly some kind of superhuman world-beating athlete (especially in the downstairs department, what kind of shape must all that be in? Jesus) and if child-bearing were an Olympic sport they'd be good for a hefty grant from Seb Coe and Co. and a gold postbox, celebrating over two decades of fallopian excellence.

However, that's me being daft. Benefits started out as a kind of insurance scheme you paid into so that when you were in the shit the government came to your rescue. Over the course of the twentieth century they mutated from this humble, sensible idea into an inalienable human right and a means to get your hands on a PlayStation. Is that what Clement Attlee had in mind? I think not. He wanted to get people back to work. Clearly he didn't get his message across.

So here we are right now in 2015 when the ConDem shower wants to bring in a benefits cap. I think this doesn't go anything like far enough. I think **a benefits cap and bells would be better**, so you could hear a benefits claimant coming from a distance and step aside, as would be polite. Shackles might also be a good addition, benefit shackles, that is, though they might get in the way when filling potholes to earn the new Scrounge Credits™ I'd be calling them if it was up to me.

If this doesn't get people back to work it might be necessary to go further. Maybe some **hole digging then filling back up again** infrastructure projects, that might work well. I wouldn't want to bring back the Workhouse, don't be absurd, not when you could house the hole-digging scrounge people in a tent or marquee. Now this might all sound a bit drastic but it'd get people back to work, wouldn't it? And there'd be plenty of new holes for landfill in case the government decides to give up on doing the bins. Which it might, especially if Sharia Law comes in, which it could, can't honestly say I know what the Koran says about the bins.

What government does: tells me not to eat chips

And this, my friends, Squires, is where the flashpoint of the twenty-first century shall be.

Not in corporations and globalization or any of that stuff. Nah! Don't be daft. Most people are smart enough to know that their mobile phone is only possible because it's made cheaply somewhere else and its signal pings off a satellite sent into space by an atmosphere-searing rocket and the body is made from plastic made from horrible oil that a million people have been killed for. Like I said, most people. So in the end we all say to ourselves ah well, not to worry and we carry on. Because we have to, because it's too late to turn any of that back and no one wants to live in a yurt with no Wi-Fi, whatever the Greens might say.

Just as the Romanovs fell in 1917 because the Russians had lost the First World War, just as the Bourbons lost their grip on French power when they called the Parlement to meet at Versailles and uncorked a half century of piled-up grievance, just as the Tower of Babel fell because mankind had built it too high and proud, so the persistent insistence by repeated bloody politicians that we should eat less chips will be the thing that in the end heralds a new dawn in these fair islands of ours.

Because if an Englishman's home is his castle, what is his plate of chips? An inviolable shrine to his place in life, his right to feed himself any way he likes, without interference from the outside world. Make not windows into men's souls and whatever you do don't lecture them about chips. Why? Because we like chips. Chips are British. They're not fries, wedges, frites, French fries or any of that and they're not crisps either. **They're chips. And they belong to us.**

Oh, and don't tell me it's the Doctors who think we should get rid of chips. The Doctors and the scientists they make up their minds and tell us something is healthy one minute, and deadly the next. Butter, sugar, salt, they've all been given the treatment. As for fats, well, one minute they're good the next minute they're bad and smoked salmon is for ponces anyway so no

'Telling you what you want to hear'

matter what it may or may not do for my brain with its Omega 3 or whatever it's called is beside the point.

Honestly, if the powers that be want this country to become ungovernable, if they want the stout men and women of the British Isles to rise up and overthrow them, if they want anarchy, chaos and calamity to erupt then this is surely the way to go about it. If they want the jails stormed, the courts overturned, angry crowds jostling in the street baying for blood and summary justice, Parliament reduced to ash and politicians' heads on spikes on Westminster Bridge then all they have to do is carry on about chips. Because it's not like we haven't heard them, out of touch, going on about how chips are bad. The steady drip, drip of anti-chip propaganda has not gone unheeded. We will not endure another moment of it.

Every chip eaten is an act of defiance, an act of rebellion, every chip eaten is the chip-eater saying: No, enough, this will not stand, you may have stripped me of my rights, done in trial by jury, extended police powers to hold suspects for fourteen days without charge, ditched habeas corpus, the right to silence, double jeopardy, the Royal Navy, shipped our gold to America for eff all, shattered our pension system, locked the NHS into hock for multiple generations, opened the floodgates of immigration, surrendered power to Brussels, dragged us through two pointless wars in the last decade or so, let the country slither into being a debauched paedo's paradise while covering it up, tried to curtail freedom of speech at every turn, snooped at our emails, spunked billions propping up banks that had gone haywire purely because you'd let them, cut back services left right and centre, poured billions into quantitative easing that goes nowhere other than to the rich, put speed cameras absolutely everywhere! But what you will not take from me, **what you shall never prise from my cold dead hands is my chips**.

Be warned, Westminster. We are ready to break. Primed to snap. Mark my words.

No no, no no no no, no no no no, no no there's no limits

So these five things that government does clearly matter, and they also mark quite clearly the **limits of what governments can and can't do**, what they can get away with, and may help you understand why, if it were down to me, there would be a Minister of Supply who would ensure that every household in the country got free chips, even the people bedding down for the night in the Work Marquees up and down the country. Because government can only be by the consent of the governed, and at no point did we consent to having our chips taken off us.

For when you're out of ideas

GREAT BRITONS

NO. 88: SRALAN 'LORD' SUGAR

Sralan is one of the world's most successful businessmen, which is why he himself bases himself in Slough. You might think it's for the attractive town centre, but he's outwitted you yet again. The man is a visionary and can clearly foresee some sort of cataclysm that will engulf everything within the M25 but leave Maidenhead and surrounding areas largely untouched. Besides, if it does all kick off in the Big Smoke he will have been alerted on his state-of-the-art webphone which once synced with specialist software and connected through the unique Ethernet socket, and providing that whoever makes the call also has the same model of webphone with the latest operating system fully installed, should be able to receive texts up to five days after they are sent.

Sralan isn't just a visionary in the business sense, he's a genuine, bona fide, salt-of-the-earth mystic. He was blessed from an early age with the ability to predict the future of people's relationships, the future of people's pets but sadly not the future of outmoded technology. Proof of this occult past exists everywhere, most obviously in his company name 'AMSTRAD' which clearly stands for AMalgamated Sralan Tarot Readings And Devil-expelling. A mate of mine said he didn't want to put the 'e' on the end as he thought AMSTRADE sounded too egotistical. He's helped so many people by predicting their future that he even gained the nickname 'Lord Sugar'. Apparently his gift is so strong, many believe that he may have created life itself. In the very strict sense he has, as he's sired three children. If you're still sceptical in the face of such overwhelming evidence then I would simply ask you this question. If he wasn't a sorcerer, why would he call his show *The Apprentice?*

GLOBAL POLITICAL IDEAS

The British political system is the best in the world, actually. The surest way to double check this is to take a look at what else is on offer around the world and go from there. Here are some of the world's political philosophies in some **Common Sense** nutshells.

France

Liberty, fraternity (brotherhood, I think) and equality. Just like the French to spell out exactly what they're not interested in really, which is fags, booze, shagging.

United States of America

Life, Liberty and the Pursuit of Happiness: grow up. Life is a series of endless relentless grinding disappointments. Dreamers.

Germany

Whatever we do we're not doing that again.*

*. . . and one World Cup. Can't help myself.

Cover yourself up Mr Putin

Russia

никто не любит нас, и мы не заботимся: [*trans*] No one likes us and we don't care.

Belgium

Do we even need a government?

Holland

Basically, do what you like but don't make a mess.

Italy

We can process that cash for you, yes.

Greece

'Neither a lender nor a borrower be, sucker'
Shakespeare.

Sweden

Listen, this place is a paradise where Swedish men and women want for nothing and live in harmony, but that beer will cost you twelve quid.

Switzerland

Listen, this place is a paradise where Swiss men and women and no one else want for nothing and live in harmony, but that beer will cost you eighteen quid.

Spain

Spain once ruled a global empire the envy of the world. Since then it's all been downhill. No idea what that must be like.

Libya

Good question.

Egypt

It's the army, stupid.

Libya

Look, give it five years.

China

The true and noble aim of Maoist-Marxist-Sino-Communist thought is to free the worker by making him work really bloody hard in a corrugated-iron warehouse churning out tat for the decadent Western imperialist running-dog lackeys and then buying their Volkswagens off them in large amounts! China will not fail! No complaining!

North Korea

외국 악마 를 화나게: [*trans*] Upset the foreign devil.

Japan

No, we won't be doing that again, either. いいえ、我々は再びそれを行うことはありません, 必ず and/or 特にサッカーで (especially at football).

South Africa

It is every South African man's inalienable right to shoot his girlfriend while she's on the toilet.

Australia

Fair go, mate, this place is full up.

New Zealand

One ring to rule them all and one ring to bind them.

Canada

OK, sounds reasonable, no problem.

Iran

The Islamic Revolution will not be televised, or allowed on Facebook.

Brazil

No idea. Seems unlikely they even have a government.

Venezuela

¡Ay carumba! Oil! Socialism for all after I've banked these billions, comrades! Who needs toilet paper anyway! After the revolution we will shit gold!

Scratching Britain's itch

FREE YOUR MIND AND THE REST WILL FOLLOW

Let Freedom ring.   Martin Luther King.

This must have been before texting.

'Do you really think you are free?' This is the kind of question those lads in Guy Fawkes masks ask. They all wear those masks to show how individual they are by the way. And possibly because they pong and know it.

Thing is, though, as much as it pains me to agree with this bunch of strokers, we are no longer free. Oh we were once. Yes we were free. Back at some point in the past that I can't quite pin down and about which I'll get back to you later, we were truly free people, who walked hand in hand with liberty, in sunlit uplands of freedom and, er, liberty, British weather permitting. We could do what we wanted, how we wanted with whomsoever we wanted. I mean, up to a point, but you get my point. We could say whatever we liked. But now, you can't do whatever you want, and you certainly can't say anything any more.

Health and Safety gone mad

But that's all gone now thanks to things like Health and Safety gone mad. I mean, I know that the hot tap is hot. I know it's hot and if I stick my hands under it I will move them away from the hot water before they are scalded. Don't treat me like a fool. I know that that ladder is high up and I might fall off it. I know. I know this and I am not an idiot. I know that I might drown in the canal, that's why I jumped in it. I'm so alone.

So-called Human Rights

But now we've got these so-called Human Rights it means we can't do what we want when we want how we want. This is because we have never had Human Rights in this country, we've just had the law.

English law is pretty much a long **can't do list**, a list compiled largely by a thing called **precedent**, which basically means until someone has done the terrible thing no one had thought of doing there was nothing to stop you doing it. What that tells you is every single illegal thing in the Common Law was done by someone, once, without any legal comeback. In other words every law basically consists of someone saying 'OH FOR GOD'S SAKE WHAT DID YOU DO THAT FOR????' and then it being made illegal. On the plus side it also means if you really use your imagination you might end up creating a new crime by accident. Everyone likes a challenge.

But Human Rights law from Europe is the other way round. It's not what you can't do, it's the **stuff you're kind of allowed to do. Why be specific?** The answer to 'FOR GOD'S SAKE WHAT DID YOU DO THAT FOR????' is no longer a swift new law followed by an equally swift conviction, instead it's: 'I fancied it and anyway I'm allowed to aren't I hang on let's check with the European Court.' So we have a proper collision between **how things are done here**, and **how they're done over there**. Recipe for disaster. And legal fees.

<u>My rights</u>

And as exciting as Human Rights are to lawyers on an hourly rate, everyone knows Human Rights aren't a patch on MY RIGHTS, and the fact that

I KNOW MY RIGHTS SO FUCK OFF, COPPER.

Yes, it's quite beautiful isn't it? This is one of the most powerful arguments surrounding rights known to man, and has been with us since time immemorial. Always rendered more powerful and refined by shouting, pointing and cider. This noble battle-cry

sounds across the annals of history and will echo long
after we are all gone.

You can't say anything any more, can you?

And then there's political correctness. You can't say
anything any more. Now, I am not afraid to say the
unsayable, even though the problem with saying the
unsayable is once you've said it, it has become said and
therefore obviously wasn't unsayable in the first place.
Also, the trouble with that is that a lot of the unsayable
used to be unsaid so it's quite hard to keep track of
what actually is unsayable. Got it? But the truth is you
can't say anything any more.

Except you can, I just did, but you know what I
mean. You simply can't say what you want any more.
You can't even say the things you wouldn't ever want to
say, under any circumstances whatsoever, any more. I
mean, you can't go into a pub in Brixton and say
something that will definitely get your head kicked in
any more. Is that the country we want to live in?

Is that the country we want to live in?

No, not me. That's not what two World Wars* and all
those other wars that get lumped in with the Second
World War to make them sound OK were fought for. So

*And one World Cup. Told you it was a reflex.

the thing is we should be able to say the unsayable, whether we want to or not, or whether there's no point to saying it other than starting a ruck. It's a matter of principle, or maybe bloody-mindedness, you know sometimes it's hard to tell the difference. The truth is we should be allowed to say what we like but we can't. Not any more, not after thirteen years of New Labour Tony Brown soft soap followed up by five years of teary-eyed Lib Dem smoothie-faced Tory coalition.

But fear not, the Guv'nor is here, and tooled up with a **Common Sense** solution to taking our freedom back.

Eight magic words

So, depressing as it is, we are no longer truly free, tangled up as we are in a web of competing restrictions on our freedom. But I have the solution. I offer you eight magic words, **eight magic words which will enable you to say or do whatever you like**.

These magic words are in use all over the world and you know what, I don't see why everyone shouldn't make use of them. It's only fair. These words mean you can do anything you like, no matter how vile, appalling, amoral, immoral, disgusting, degrading or perverted, and you can get off scot-free. You might even find that if you're lucky other people start saying it for you and you don't have to apologize. They'll do it for you.

These eight magic words are better than Charlie Bucket's Gold Ticket, better than a fancy silk, better than a secret identical twin who you keep in a cellar for those tricky DNA database moments. No one can touch you, and the likes of the *Guardian* will run an editorial saying it's not your fault anyway.

They're even better than saying you're disaffected, which used to be the card you'd get out if you wanted to do something terrible. Only problem with that is then they'd try to teach you to read or play table tennis in a community centre. These magic words mean you don't have to do any of that stuff, you'll never have to play ping-pong in a room with broken central heating as penance. Ever. Eight magic words!

How powerful? This powerful

Eight magic words, **eight words more powerful** even than '**I love you**'. Sweeter to say than '**I told you so**'. Such is the magic in these words. For we know 'I love you' are the three most powerful words the world has known up to this point: deploy those words at the wrong time and you could end up losing half your CD collection. 'I told you so' are **the four sweetest words** in the English language, as any woman can tell you, gents, you don't need fine wine or words, nor a working knowledge of erogenous zones to get a woman to the point of orgasm where her soul soars like an eagle and touches the Elysian Fields of pleasure themselves,* no: all you need do is something **mildly disappointing** you've been previously warned against, she gets to say 'I told you so' and boom! she's got her jollies and you can go back to the shed and **work on your model railway**.

<u>Prepare to be liberated</u>

So these words are incredibly powerful, and I'm sure you'll agree that in a fair and free world everyone should have access to these words, for without them we are living at a permanent, unfree disadvantage. To be free we must have these words for ourselves and learn to use them.

So here they are, and this is how you use them. Do the terrible thing you want to do then simply say who you are and then pronounce:

'NO: THIS IS THE WAY OF MY PEOPLE'

and that way no one can touch you. You can do what you want, blow people up, fly planes into things, cut people's heads off, punch women in the face, string people up, disembowel people you disagree with, chuck 'em off buildings, set fire to them, lop bits off people

*I've read about it.

who've got the wrong hat on. Fill your boots! Be as bad as you want to be!

This is true freedom, better than anything enshrined in law or Magna Carta or certainly that European Human Rights Bloody Thing or any of that stuff, because it's freedom without responsibility. Jackpot! Who could ask for anything more?

Unsqueezing the middle

MEN OF THE MOMENT: DAVID CAMERON

'Who is pulling the strings?' by John Owens of the RSWP, the Radical Socialist Workers Party (Unemployed Cadre)

Thank you, Comrades.

Five years-ish now this man has been our so called Prime Minister in a government that was UNELECTED by the British people who could not vote Labour for lack of a serious leftist post-Maoist option but now is not the time for that story of outright betrayal! Yet who is he? What – if anything – can be known about him?

A great deal, as it happens.

Well, he's a Tory, of course. That means he must be several things automatically. Evil. A bastard. Out for his Tory mates. Evil. Vermin. Yes. Vermin. Parasitical vermin. Or a parasite on vermin. Whichever is worse.

And who can argue with any of that? But who is he really?

Well, he's a ham-faced, gammon-cheeked, pork-foreheaded, blushing slab of bacon. That much is certain. A plum with a nose, a melon that's gone off. A basketball, painted red, that has been deflated a bit and looks like a gammon. You get the picture.

It is a matter of public record that he went to Eton College, the ultimate incubator for Toffs, where braying classes are compulsory and the cadet force does bayonet practice on the poor on Bank Holidays. Oh yes, celebrating the banks getting a day off from feasting on ordinary working people's efforts. During his time at Eton, students would often be woken in the middle of the night to grenade nearby council estates and deliver jack-booted top-hatted class war to the unsuspecting proletariat of Slough. There are no records of this because the police, in the pay of the Thatcher government at the time, covered it up. But enough of his upbringing.

He's hell-bent on trying to starve as many children as he possibly can by any means possible. That is also incontrovertible. Every child that starves makes him happy. Vermin, remember?

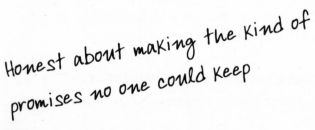

Honest about making the kind of promises no one could keep

He has sold all of the NHS off to his mates for peanuts so they can drink the blood of the sick and wipe their arses with fivers paid for by the terminally ill. We know that. Leeches.

What was he before he was a politician? He was a PR man. Not a miner. Not a docker. Not a ship's steward. But a PR man. For ITV no less, their Carlton wing. Commercial television, the beacon of capitalist, consumerist hate-speak rather than the disappointingly soft-left BBC. Spending his days coming up with slogans for *Emmerdale* and *Coronation Street*, the very propaganda that has been used to gull and lull the working people of this country into somnambulant acquiescence with every new amoral Tory outrage, not living amongst real people with real lives living in a real way. Ask ourselves this, brothers and sisters: can we really trust a man who wrote the press releases for things like *Alphabet Castle*, *Brighton Belles*, *Catchphrase* (once Carlton had stolen it off Meridian), *The Good Sex Guide*, *Goodnight Mister Tom* (racist!), *Inspector Morse*, *The Hypnotic World of Paul McKenna*, *Talking Telephone Numbers*, *TV's Naughtiest Blunders* and *Scavengers* with John Leslie? No, comrades, we cannot. That first episode of *Scavengers* failed to deliver the thrills promised in Mr Cameron's silver-tongued press release. When time is precious on the march to revolution that was a precious hour I will never get back.

So what does he stand for? Apart from his City banker pals, who he's been propping up since the very moment he drew breath? He does nothing to create any other impression. Equal marriage was a bourgeois smoke screen for which he deserves no credit. Vermin often do what they can to appear cuddly.

Well there is more to David Cameron than meets the eye. For the truth is he has been hiding a very real secret from the British public, one that if the world knew, the world would recoil in horror, then pity, then back to horror. Neither of these go down that well at the ballot box so you can see why he might have kept his secret so, erm, secret.

For while it is true that endless strings have been pulled for David Cameron to get to where he is in British politics today, David Cameron *himself* has being pulling strings. Strings he's pulled all his life. Strings he had to pull or he wouldn't be standing at the Despatch Box in the House of Fools. Hard hitting.

For what we don't know about David Cameron but we ought to, is whether in fact he is simply a head – a gammon, ham-like head – with a tiny body, little dangly arms and miniature legs, sat in a moleskin saddle atop the shoulders of a loyal gamekeeper's son, whom DC operates by a system of strings and pulleys. Cameron's tiny reins are attached to his human beast of burden's ears, he pulls left for left, right for right, jabs his diamond-encrusted spurred ankles into his neck to get him to wave his arms, whatever. How else do you explain how the man moves?

We should be told whether this is the case. Numerous Freedom of Information requests filed by our party have come to nothing. Typical. Indeed, the last phone call I made was met with laughter. The laughter of what? Parasitical vermin leeches.

It may or may not be true. But this is not the point. As the Nazi-fascist warlord and warmonger Winston Churchill once said, though he made a good point so I will attribute it: 'a lie is halfway around the world before the truth has got its boots on'. He said a lot else besides, much of it Nazi and fascist, but what we can learn from this is if we start a rumour about David Cameron being some sort of portable cranium man, literally standing on the shoulders of the ordinary working man, a working man bent double with the effort of carrying his so-called master, kicked in the neck by the pork-chopped ham-faced aristo who is laughing and loving every second of it then maybe people will see him for what he really is/might be/isn't but it's a good metaphor.

And what is truth anyway? It's another construct devised by right-wing academics to suppress thinking and independent thought.

Get this story out there, comrades and it will deliver the final fatal blow that the bloated corpse of Labour – about whom sadly I have neither time nor the word count permitted, and trust me I have a great deal to say about the Labour Party, comrades – has so far failed to deliver even as the Tory Party with its coalition gimp buddies staggers from disaster to disaster.

Tell your friends, tell your co-workers and/or co-benefits claimants – and I have to stress that we in the RSWP judge no one, friends – that David Cameron is the string-pulling disembodied head man, who sleeps in a Moses basket and eats rusks for breakfast.

Tell them that, and whether it is true or not – and who knows in the current web of Westminster lies, it may well be? – and the public will see the Tories for what they really are, or might be, it doesn't matter. Do what must be done. The future will thank you for it even as it lauds its own generations of revolutionaries.

Thank you for listening. Tomorrow is ours.

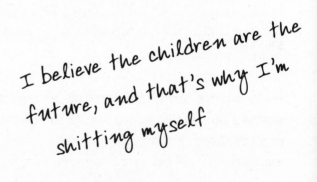

I believe the children are the future, and that's why I'm shitting myself

THE INTERNET

The best argument against democracy is a five-minute conversation with the average voter. **Winston Churchill**, who'd never been on Twitter

So the internet, right? What the hell do we do about that, Squire? Because if ever there was stable door that can't be locked now that the porny horse has bolted it's the internet.

What I won't do is treat you like some kind of simpleton and remind you of how we the British invented the World Wide Web, as well as the computer which was invented by an autistic Benedict Cumberflap angling for an Oscar as Best British Homosexual. You know that already and to bang on about it would be inappropriate, though it is worth remembering. And that it won us the war. Hands down. On our own. Germans never guessed we were reading their stuff. But we shouldn't bang on about it.

The internet is truly amazing, you can't deny it. In many ways it is truly miraculous. It connects people with the rest of the world, brings like minds together, enables them to share their interests, pics, wank etc. and then the police can nick them.

Modern technology has been accused of causing a breakdown in communication within families. The sort of people who say this have never tried talking to a teenager. They're not interested. Or interesting. Let them get on with it, I say.

No, the internet and modern communications present anyone trying to get to grips with what is going wrong with the country with a very serious set of problems. It's undermining everything. You only have to look at the frothing shoals of muppets and morons on the likes of Twitter to make you wonder whether it wouldn't be better to hand the world over to the cockroaches formally and nuke ourselves into oblivion. Facebook has brought people together all over the world, allowing them to realize what a tedious thing it is to be human and how desperate we are to offload some of that tedium on to others.

More than that, though, everyone has an opinion. Now, you might say, Guv'nor that's not necessarily a bad thing, but seeing as I am the only person who is reliably right about anything, it *is* actually a bad thing, and unnecessary. And as if the inane chatter and pictures of knobs and the rest wasn't bad enough, the internet means if you go online you pretty quickly find yourself dealing with the kind of people you'd cross the street to assault.

Thought is the enemy of reason

But in these times of Terror and Jihadi threat the internet is a serious issue for us all. It's a question of freedom, freedom of speech and a right to privacy.

Now: privacy matters to you and me the freeborn peoples of these islands. Indeed, I would say that privacy is a paramount right and one we would barter away at our peril. If I sit on the toilet, perhaps to spend a leisurely amount of time to myself, so to speak, it's no one's business. That's privacy. But if I sit on the toilet in order to give the appearance of spending a leisurely amount of time to myself, so to speak, but am in fact plotting blowing something up or the destruction of The West, then I should without a doubt be stopped. And that's the reason we installed CCTV in the Ladies in my pub; it's in my statement and I really shouldn't say any more about that.

The Secret Service and GCHQ want to read our emails, apparently. Well I have nothing to hide. And you have nothing to hide. And if you have nothing to hide you have nothing to worry about. Anyway, when I want to discuss changing the sell-by dates on crisps I always make sure that I have the radio turned up really loud as well as a shower running so no one can hear me. You can't be too careful.

Of course, this would suggest that the Secret Service and GCHQ and MI19 (yes, they're up to nineteen now) know how email works. Well, the fact is no one does, no one knows how it works, nobody has a faintest idea, least of all the tech guy at your office, so if they are going to read people's emails they must have some very clever people on it, clever people who know what they're doing. The trouble with clever people, though, is they can start having doubts and wobble and do spectacularly stupid things, like that treacherous little shit Snowden.

But what you have to understand about the internet and Terror is this: there are precious freedoms at stake. Precious freedoms some of which we didn't know we had until very recently. **These precious new freedoms include:**

- ✗ the precious freedom to go online on social media when we are shit-faced;
- ✗ and call a minor celebrity 'has been cunt' for instance;
- ✗ or say 'your a fat bold twatt';
- ✗ or say 'Who r u? Id rather shit in me hands than wotch u';
- ✗ or just 'fukk of'.

And when terror threatens such precious delicate freedoms we must tread carefully.

Because it is precisely these kind of sweet, sweet freedoms that our Jihadi enemies despise, because they are jealous of such noble freedoms. It is these freedoms they want to destroy, as well as a lot of other ones obviously, so if we stop people saying unimaginative tedious crude things to strangers online because they're bored, drunk or lonely then the terrorists will have won. But the Jihadis and their ilk take advantage of these very freedoms and use those freedoms to attack those same freedoms . . .

Look, it's complicated, OK? It's a riddle inside a conundrum wrapped in a puzzle behind a firewall. But we have to do something, and I actually think a double-whammy-joined-up-two-birds-one-stone-Common-Sense-thinking solution is on offer. And not just deleting your browsing history before the wife gets in or using more than one password for everything. No: we have to do more than that.

Radical measures are called for. So, what we do is:

✗ Turn off the internet at 5 p.m. every Friday evening.
✗ Turn it back on 9 a.m. Monday morning.

The benefits would be:

✗ no more drunk tweeting;
✗ no more vengeful emails to the ex;
✗ no more impulse purchases on Amazon;
✗ an end to desperate attempts to cancel impulse purchases on Amazon;
✗ no more having to use In Private Browsing or

whatever it's called as you cry hot lonely tears in your bedsit;

✗ no more watching compilations of air-crashes;

✗ no more visiting sites you really shouldn't to see things no man or woman can possibly un-see, ruining the mood at Sunday lunch.

Furthermore it would also:

✗ reduce the possibility of terror plotting and/or attack at the weekends, which will help the emergency services perform their proper function, helping Britain's patriotic drinkers get home/ patched up.

And if that makes me a totalitarian then so be it.

'Common sense party for common sensible people.'

TRANSPORT – MOVING BRITAIN FORWARD (SLIGHT TAILBACK)

Britain's transportation system – which was once the envy of the world – has come in for some harsh criticism from many quarters over the last few years. There are many theories as to why this is: creeping privatization; lack of government funding; the fact that it's shit.

Let's take the railways for starters. We invented the railways, the rest of world copied them, but ever since Dr Beeching took a knife to the network fifty years ago, Britain's railways have struggled to maintain standards set during the glory days of Brunel, George Stephenson and the 'This is the age of the train' Intercity adverts, featuring a person I've been advised against mentioning.*

*Clunk click every trip? No thanks, pal. I don't wear a seat-belt any more because I'd rather fly through a windscreen and be lacerated by shattering glass and land under a lorry's wheels than be told what to do by a nonce. And it wasn't the age of the train we should have all been worrying about. Thanks a lot, *Panorama*.

Gone are the days when you could buy a thickish cardboard ticket, board a train with a potentially dangerous slam-shut door, purchase a can of McEwan's Export and relax in the company of fellow travellers, smoking themselves stupid. Salad days, indeed. It was called second class, not standard. Because back then people knew their place.

In contrast, your modern train journey is an experience so hellish it doesn't bear thinking about. If the train isn't delayed because of staff shortages at Crewe or Michael Portillo's pink suit becoming derailed just outside Bristol Parkway, you have to put up with the nightmare that's modern technology. Gadgets have ruined what used to be a pleasant experience. The other week I was about to take a nap following my Ginsters-based luncheon, when I was rudely awoken by some tool in the seat next to me, who was watching *American Pie 9: Cremation Camp*, on their laptop. I mean, do us a favour. Everyone knows those films tailed off after the fifth one.

It's my belief that we have three options with regards sorting the railways: Firstly, we can re-nationalize them; secondly, we invest more money in the existing system; and thirdly, we learn to drive.

Another theory put forward by one distinguished expert (me) is that we grasp the nettle and nationalize Richard Branson, so he comes under state control.

This would enable us to implement the following changes:

- ✗ Everyone gets an upgrade to First Class on all Virgin Train services (free crisps and pop, no thank you I don't want a sandwich);
- ✗ Virgin Space Travel will replace capital punishment; and, finally,
- ✗ Necker Island to become a Club 18–30 resort.

'So what about the roads?' I hear you ask. Well, if the truth be told, I couldn't really give a monkey's. This isn't because of some newly found hippy-dippy, yoghurt-weaving, mung bean casserole, bicycle-riding, save the planet ideology. No, this has more to do with the fact I lost my licence a few months ago. I now get around courtesy of ABC1 Carz so I don't have to brave the potholes (see below), bus lanes, M25 long-term car park, berks who tow caravans, or any of the other nonsense the honest, road tax-paying British citizen has to deal with, day in, day out.

Then there are those who say we should seek a Green solution to our transport problems. Poppycock and balderdash, is what I say to that. If the Greens had their way, we'd all be cycling around on roads made from hemp, towing our kids in one of those rickety-looking trailers, and doing our food shopping at a vegan hypermarket which doesn't approve of plastic bags or sell Fray Bentos pies.

I mean, these loonies want to bring back canals. I mean canals, for heaven's sakes – instead of roads! You tell me how they intend hosting our bit of the Tour de France on a canal – tow paths simply aren't wide enough for drug-fuelled super-athletes and all those nutters who run in front of the cyclists. Oh, and you tell me how ITV2 staple *Police Camera Action!* can continue to exist in a canal-based setting? No one's going to watch a copper pull a barge over for exceeding the speed limit of 3 m.p.h. past moored vessels. **Common Sense** tells you it's doomed to failure.

The 10-Point Common Sense Guide to Improving Transport

- ✔ All forms of transport will be free at point of delivery

- ✔ Forget that – got it muddled up with the NHS

- ✔ Daft American term 'train station' to be replaced with the more traditional British 'railway station'

- ✔ The Michael Portillo gravy train to be substituted by a replacement bus service

- ✔ Toll roads which don't actually exist, to be made free

- ✔ Third runway to be built on Heathrow's second runway

- ✔ HS2 to be scrapped in favour of a twice-daily Megabus service

- ✔ Eurostar to concentrate on its vital London-to-Kent services

- ✔ Student Railcard to be replaced by a Live In The Real World, Full Fare, Get Over Yourself, You Have No Idea How Lucky You Really Are Rail Pass

- ✔ Cycle lanes to be replaced by something more useful or at least paved with cobbles for laughter value

Potholes

Potholes are an indication of the moment when civilization starts to come undone. Potholes in the highway are the road-based equivalent of dotting the is and crossing the ts.

This is why they annoy people: they make us think the government has forgotten about us, that the government doesn't care. Every pothole you clunk your front wheel into is the government flicking a V at you. It's the Tory front bench shrugging at you. It's Ed Miliband laughing at you with that weird forced laugh of his. **It's Poor Nick Clegg staring at the carpet opposite him dreaming of his wife's paella.** OK, so it's the council's responsibility, but that's not the point. Every pothole is a step towards chaos, a reminder that the powers that be simply don't care.

So what to do? Get rid of Trident to pay for sorting out potholes? No, don't be daft. Submarines are cool.

Simple. All MPs have to go on weekly pothole patrol. When they find a pothole they have to stand next to it with a flag, waving it around like a marshal in the F1, whatever the weather. This will work on the principle of the Third Rule of **Common Sense**: **'How Does It Affect Me?'** because there's no way MPs will put up with having to do that for more than a couple of weeks: they'll prioritize sorting out potholes in a flash rather than stand in the pissing rain.

Tough on the causes of causes

THE BEAUTIFUL BRITISH CRIMINAL MIND

By crime expert, Maltese Andy

They only harmed their own – Ron & Reg, Better Times

Before I go any further, let me point out that I in no way condone violence (OK, maybe just a slap, watch yourself) and may I also point out that I renounce criminality in any way, shape or form. Including that time we did that jewellers in Stratford on scooters. I was lost, confused by the one-way system, and was on my way back from clay pigeon shooting and had a problem with the safety catch on my shotgun.

What I'd like to say is this: The hardworking, taxpaying, upstanding, law-abiding, boring citizens are the very foundations on which any society is built. Whereas ponces, grasses and nonces provide the foundations for flyovers and motorway bridges.

Britain has produced some of the most iconic villains over the years – faces who have managed to pull off some of the biggest jobs in the history of taking stuff that doesn't belong to you. This is no fluke. It's usually a result of precise planning, cool heads, that fat security guard taking a bung and plod being a bit slow off the mark. The Great Train Robbery of 1963 in which a gang robbed a Royal Mail train of £2.6m is a prime example of ingenuity, daring and grievous bodily harm coming together, resulting in the perfect blag. To put that figure in perspective, if that mob had pulled the same job today, they'd have got away with £48 mil., 7,500 Amazon parcels and 128,000 pieces of junk mail. Tasty.

Then there was the job in Hatton Garden back in 1978, which I only found out about when I read the papers the following day because I was in all night with the missus, watching television, so I was nowhere near the place. They had it away with hundreds of thousands of pounds' worth of sparklers, and no one got hurt – not even the shop owner who ended up in hospital with concussion.

With your British criminal, it's just business – professional, like. Whereas with your foreign criminal I'm afraid we're talking amateur night. Those mugs are more than likely to panic, shit themselves, involve civilians, grass everyone up and eventually get shot by Gene Hackman trying to escape on a boat, like that bloke did at the end of *French Connection II*. Can you imagine that sort of thing happening to Ronnie Biggs? He'd have been away on his toes, and sunning himself on Copacabana Beach before you could say 'extradition treaty'. The Brink's-Mat boys – no one even knows who they are what they done or whether they even done it, let alone how much gold was actually in that van.

Politicians have never really understood the British criminal mentality, which is why I won't have it when people slag off the likes of Jonathan Aitken, Jeffrey Archer and Lord Taylor of Warwick. OK, they was guilty of their crimes and betrayed the trust of the British people, but they could also be seen as parliamentary visionaries who were fully committed to finding out what life was like on the wrong side of the tracks, and discovering for themselves what it's like to have to crap in a bucket.

That's why we don't want any foreign criminals coming over here, because they give crime a bad name. For every ponce, paedo, rapist, double murderer, wife strangler, knife work expert and cash-machine cracker that comes here from Poland, Latvia, Lithuania and those other places where they teach picking pockets at school that's a British crime job taken. Gone. Never to be replaced. If some Estonian slag picks a pocket, and empties a wallet, what is left for the British criminal? Nothing. We need to take care of our own. Is that too much to ask? Or am I going to have to wire up your testicles to a field telephone and crank the handle to get an answer out of you that I like?

Now: the British criminal is a proud fellow, a man with standards. But he is also someone who respects the law, up to a point. It's an outrage that some of these crims arrive from abroad without having had their records checked, and the next thing you know some foreign bastard is flashing on a British pervert's patch without so much as a by your leave.

This is why I am one hundred per cent against Europe, except as a place to launder money quickly and easily or somewhere handy to go to ground when a blag goes wrong, not that I would know anything about that. Now, you won't hear me arguing for tightening up border controls. In fact I'd be the last person to insist on that: those arseholes in Customs can do one. But what we need is strict controls on foreign criminals, unless you need a dynamite guy from Sicily for a job, but a home-grown job, sourced here in the UK.

Summing up (a term I'm not unfamiliar with), I think what I'm trying to say is that we have an abundance of criminal talent in this country that needs protection from foreign competition. Because the British criminal mind is the greatest criminal mind in the world. And it works like this:

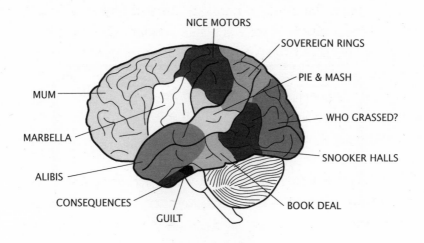

The criminal mind (British)

We don't look after our elderly enough in this country, or indeed in the care homes that we run as a business, for which I'm facing numerous criminal charges of negligence.

Simon Coldarted, CEO (suspended pending inquiry), Back to Basics Retirement Homes

DEALING WITH THE WRONG 'UNS

Law-breaking is one of the biggest causes of crime in Britain today. Going back to the year dot, man has murdered, embezzled, kidnapped and, perhaps worst of all, stolen my massive charity bottle of whisky full of shrapnel, which was sat on the end of the bar. I know who did that as well, the little scrote, but his dad and his uncle's drinking keeps me afloat midweek so there's no way I can make a fuss; he's got me over a barrel over a barrel.

Governments down the years have struggled manfully to put a stop to the runaway train that is crime. They've tried every trick in the book in the hope they can somehow halt it, or even slow it down, the Major government even going so far as to make Michael Howard Home Secretary at one time – enough to put the shits up any hardened criminal, you'd think, but no. Even putting Death's bat-man himself in charge didn't work. Theresa May might turn the souls of honest men to dust, but even she with her leopardskin shoes and penetrating gaze can't sort it. Anyway, some fellas are into that.

The Crimewave has now become seemingly relentless – on and on it goes, wrecking people's lives in its wake, tearing at the nation's very soul and seeing me pick up several points on my licence. But that's another story. Chris Huhne was driving. He can be very persuasive.

People live in fear in the shadow of crime. Analysing crime statistics points to one chilling conclusion; the law of averages clearly states that at some point you will be played by an actor who doesn't look much like you that no one will see ever again in *Crimewatch*.

And this is modern crime, by the way. Not proper old-school crime. Nowadays you'll often hear it said, mainly by older members of the *EastEnders* cast, that you could leave your door open in the old days and the Krays and the like only killed their own and loved their mum and respected their neighbours who feared them, yes, but honoured them also, and this is completely true.

So has the nation's moral compass descended into chaos created by a perfect storm of poverty, austerity and unemployment? Or is it because we're a nation of horrible toe-rags?

The great British public don't want to hear excuses, they want results and they want them pronto – a bit like *Final Score*, minus Gary Lineker and the pools panel.* There are many searching questions which need answering regarding community policing: for instance, whatever happened to the humble bobby on the beat? Whatever happened to the friendly desk sergeant? And of course whatever happened to the genial Special Branch officer posing as a striking miner?† The simple answer, my friends, is that those halcyon days which never existed have gone and we're now having to deal with it.

However, it's not all doom and gloom. Fear not, people, because I can reveal to you all that there is light at the end of the tunnel. **FUKP** have asked a group of brainboxes at the local technical college to feed the crime figures of the past ten years into a computer. They then pressed some buttons and sat around for a bit and talked about *Star Wars* and wouldn't it be nice if they had a girlfriend, before coming up with the incredible conclusions shown overleaf.

---

*By the way if the day came and I was this country's leader, I'd bring back the teleprinter to TV, they're wasting money with all that other flash stuff.
†That one's easier to answer, he'd be the only miner there was. Not the best of cover.

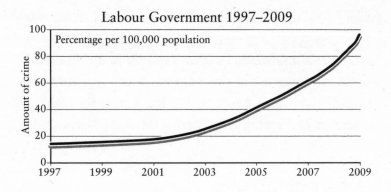

Labour Government 1997–2009

Percentage per 100,000 population

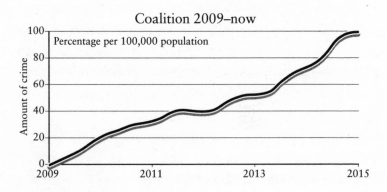

Coalition 2009–now

Percentage per 100,000 population

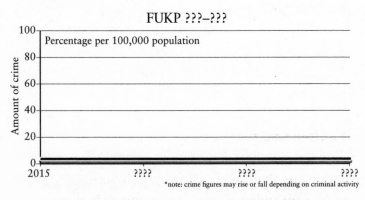

FUKP ???–???

Percentage per 100,000 population

*note: crime figures may rise or fall depending on criminal activity

How crime figures might look under FUKP

— 180 —

GREAT BRITONS

NO. 32: SIMON COWELL

Simon Cowell is a Great Briton for so many reasons, principally because of his services not to music, which are what they are and require not one more drop of spilt ink about how fucking dreadful the music is, but as the UK's greatest innovator and exporter of a new and incredibly exciting model for democracy. And while Mr Cowell and his lifestyle, his 'treatments', his high-waisted trousers, his love life and so on are targets for many a lazy jibe, we will have no truck with that here, for we come here to praise Mr Cowell, not to bury him.

It's often said that young people feel disconnected from the democratic process. And this can lead politicians then to chase the youth vote, ending up with them trying to rap or wearing daft clothes that humiliate and degrade the very soul of Parliament. (Might have gone in a bit hard there, but one of those pictures of a Cabinet minister in a baseball cap on a slow news day goes a million miles.) And no matter how hard they try it seems that young people will not connect with politics unless they're searingly un-self-aware sociopathic young Conservatives, pile-inducingly earnest young Labour activists, even more earnest and soul-shatteringly humourless mega-leftwads, little lost Liberals and lads who fancy a ruck, who end up on what's called the political fringes even though they all shave all their hair off. These young people are going to vote. They're not the issue. The issue is connecting with the 95 per cent of normal youngsters who aren't like this. And it's Mr Cowell who's done it.

For Simon Cowell has not only got the youth of today, who will be the adults of tomorrow, but also some of their mums and nans to address the most basic of democratic ideals. And he's done it here in the UK, in the United States and all over the world. He has involved people in the simple business of getting people to register their choice, via modern technology, in a way that politicians can only envy. And not only that, he's making heaps of lovely cash out of it. And unlike a democratically elected MP, he'll never have to worry about getting hauled across the coals as a result of claiming for a third diamond-encrusted Lear Jet.

Yes: Mr Cowell has done what no democracy dared ever to do. While the mighty free pluralistic democracies of the world bought these freedoms in blood, in countless human lives, in the endless struggle of ordinary people, instead the price paid for a vote in Mr Cowell's democratic utopia is 45p pleasecheckwiththepersonwhopaysyourbill, calls maycostmorefromamobilethanfromalandline. Not only that but the ancient principle of one man, one vote has been taken by Mr Cowell and expanded, enhanced and monetized further: truly this vote has the X Factor. For no longer is it one man, one vote – it's one nan, many votes, as well as mums, boys feigning no interest, dads,* all furiously voting not just once but multiple times. Every Saturday and Sunday. A vote for the plump lady who works in LIDL, who you're positive you've also seen in *Benefits Street*, needn't be just the one vote, you can vote again and again. And again. And this system shows First Past the Post, Proportional Representation, Single Transferable

*And we mustn't forget those poor waifs who've switched channels in order to escape the horror that is *The Voice*.

Vote and all other contenders a whole new and exciting way to vote. Change your mind. Vote again. Vote even after the lines are closed, you may still be charged.

Never before has voting made so much sense. Or money. And the thing is, it's not even an election for the administration, in fact no matter how many millions of votes are cast, or who you vote for, Simon Cowell always wins. There isn't a politician in the country who doesn't envy this brilliant electoral system, this beacon of democracy, this most graviest of trains. As we make our way into the twenty-first century, verily this man is a beacon of democratic change.

DREAM CABINET FOR A PERFECT WORLD

Forming a cabinet is one of the trickiest things in the world of politics. Political parties have their own problems with hierarchies, debts to be honoured and who's going to sit next to Eric Pickles's waterlogged armpits during meetings – it's a minefield. It's not always the case that someone who knows anything about Health becomes Health Minister. I wouldn't trust any of them with a bottle of Night Nurse, let alone waiting lists or patient risk management. That Lansley bloke, for instance – is he a First-Aider? Can he use online Symptom Checker? I think not.

Luckily, if the moment came and the Queen called me to Buckingham Palace and said, 'OK Guv, sort it out,' then at the drop of a hat I'd have to assemble a cabinet in a hurry. And having no actual party members, apart from the members of the Drink Tank, Steve, Steve, Alan and Steve, I can therefore assemble a cabinet from anyone I like. Though I think we'd draw the line at reanimating Churchill, besides, even a zombie Churchill would probably make a leadership bid. He had form on that score you know.

So:

Chancellor of the Exchequer: Jimmy Carr

Ministers for Tax: Take VAT

Deputy PM: Nick Clegg, just to watch him suffer

Foreign Secretary: Mrs Farage, she's foreign and she's a secretary

Home Secretary: Kirsty Young and Martin Bayfield off *Crimewatch*

Archbishop of Canterbury: Dickie Dawkins, that'll learn him

Speaker of the House of Commons: Jeremy Kyle, he's made for that job

Education Secretary: chosen at random on social media; person whose messages contain the most spelling mistakes gets the job

Defence Minister: Brian Moore. No one would mess with us would they?

Minister for Sport: Gary Lineker, top bloke

Minister for Crisps: Lineker again

Secretary of State for Health: Charlie off *Casualty*

First Minister for Norwich: Alex Salmond, so he can learn what it's actually like to be ignored by the rest of the UK

My Personal Bodyguard: Gemma Arterton, Abbey Clancy, Freida Pinto, Myleene Klass, Jayne Secker off Sky News

Secretary of State for Being in a State: Shane MacGowan

Minister Without Portfolio: Uh?

Secretary of State for Wales: Do me a favour

Minister for Food, Agriculture & Swearing: Gordon Ramsay

Standing up to Brussels one banana at a time

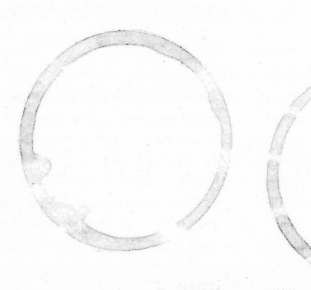

FUKP FACT UP: BRITAIN V. EUROPE (MARKS OUT OF 10)

If whether we go in or out of Europe is the big issue this year, it's best to have all the facts, all the information at our fingertips to be able to make a balanced and rational assessment of exactly what's at stake. Facts, like hips, don't lie. So, let's take a level-headed and balanced look at the facts of **BRITAIN** v. EUROPE.

Politics: Churchill (GB) v. Hitler (Europe)

Big Win scored a big win over his 5'1" German adversary, leading the good bits of the world to a second successive victory over the continental troublemakers. The cigar-smoking legend with a natty turn of phrase and granite cojones the size of Norfolk was voted Greatest Ever Briton – which means, logically, that he is also Greatest Ever Human. Hitler led probably the most evil regime in history, and ended his life by treating his young wife Eva to unquestionably the worst honeymoon ever. No contest. As if you needed to ask:

Verdict: **Britain 10** Europe 0

Making stuff: Isambard Kingdom Brunel (GB) v Ernie Rubik (Europe)

Brunel was the legendary pin-up boy of nineteenth-century mechanical and civil engineering, banging out classic feats of constructional wizardry as if they were peanut butter sandwiches – bridges, railways, tunnels, ships, hospitals and, on one occasion, a machine for attempting to extract a coin from his own windpipe. Long story. Turned out he just needed to stand on his head. Live and learn. The man was a certifiable genius. Half-French, his British half was spurred into compensating and did so gloriously. Rubik was also a talented inventor and architect. Who for some reason devoted himself to inventing a toy cube so difficult as to be of interest only to complete losers. Timewasters never win.

Verdict: **Britain 10** Europe 0

Culture: Shakespeare (GB) v. Ace of Base (Europe)

Number-one-ranked playwright of both the sixteenth and seventeenth centuries, Shakespeare churned out hit after hit after hit. And he did not just find a winning formula and crank it out over and over again. He mastered many styles – the rom-com, the rom-trag, the all-action blockbuster, the historical mockumentary, and the teenage sex romp. Ace of Base might proudly claim to be Sweden's third most successful band ever, but their global smash-hit single 'All That She Wants', about a woman who wants another baby, prompted a generation of benefit-scrounging single mothers expecting to be funded by the state. Catchy, though.

Verdict: **Britain 10** Europe 1

Sport: Bobby Charlton (GB) v. Libor Němeček (Europe)

Sir Bobby Charlton is universally revered as one of the greatest footballers of all time. He was the pile-driving heartbeat of England's 1966 World Cup winners, his nation's record goal-scorer, survivor of a thirty-year comb-over, and a legendary figure whose brilliance over almost two decades at Manchester United helped transform his club into a globally renowned brand, renowned across the whole globe. In short, Charlton was and remains a global icon whose renowned fame transcended his sport. Němeček, by contrast, was a 1990s Czech tennis player whose career peak was a first-round exit in the 1990 Australian Open, and who reached a highest ranking of 164 in the world in 1992, before sinking into obscurity. Is this the best Europe has got to offer?

Verdict: **Britain 10** Europe 0

Food: British sausage v. Bratwurst

No contest. The holy British sausage, cooked to a recipe handed down from King Arthur himself, is a fundamental expression of what it means to be British, in a convenient finger-roll-compatible format. Its continental cousin is mashed up tube of testicles. Which is fine if you like that kind of thing which no one does except people who are in the grip of the deepest darkest self-loathing i.e. the Germans.

Verdict: **Britain 10** Europe 0

FINAL SCORE:
Britain 50
EUROPE 1

HOW TO DEBATE AND DEFINITELY ALWAYS WIN ARGUMENTS

Debate is an important part of the political process. And the truth is no one really knows how to do it any more.

What you're meant to do is offer the argument for, the argument against and then decide which is the better argument.

And there's the problem, instantly. What's the good of that? You want to win the argument, not decide which is the better argument.

So, here's how it's done. And to demonstrate how effective this technique is I will use the most complex modern political problem facing the world right now: the Euro Crisis.

The euro: what the how?

The euro is the biggest problem currently facing our end of the world (you'll notice I didn't say Europe. Why would I?)

Things have got so bad the world is looking to the **Germans for leadership** and the **French for moral courage**. Now that's a fuck up whichever way you cut it.

And the thing is no one can explain exactly what's gone wrong. It's complex. Enormous. Involves economics blah blah.

So this is where my **win any argument** technique comes in.

Basically what you do is this. Start up a conversation about the euro. For instance: '**Here, what's going on with the euro, eh?**' – you can make up your own version but this seems as good a place as any to start.

And they say something like: '**Well, er, the Germans want their money back?**'

So what you do is pause, wait, look them in the eye, take a breath and say: '**No, it's much more complicated than that.**'

And that way you get to appear to be cleverer than them and win the argument. Every single time.

It never fails. If your hypothetical euro debater had said:

'. . . well, what we have here is the failure of a macro economic system that was born largely of political over confidence and complacency in Europe's political classes, trying to force through a form of fiscal union without the political union needed to pull it off, for a variety of conflicting reasons, relying on crossing their fingers and hoping for the best. After all, the Germans were bound to be confident what with their own successful adoption of a single currency after reunification, the Ost mark being bought for one Deutsch mark showing the way in currency union, but without taking into account the simple lack of centrality that a European currency would have – necessarily. After all, separate sovereign governments are hardly going to surrender control of their budgets to a central European government, especially not when the differing economies are as diverse as they are, as well as being in differing states of their respective economic cycles, and subject to democratic change: governments making promises they can keep locally but not internationally. But the French, seeing the success of the German economy wanted to have a slice of that action, rolled out the idea of a one size fits all currency, then allowed in former Communist states, new to both the free market and democracy, which were ill-equipped to withstand the shocks and strains of being at the bottom of the pile euro-wise. And without a central enforceable set of fiscal rules – which of course everyone knows they need to make the currency work but which of course they will never agree to – basically the whole Jerry-built thing will eventually be torn apart by its own contradictions because no one actually thought it through on any level whatsoever . . .'

You pause, wait, look them in the eye, take a breath and say: **'No, it's much more complicated than that.'**

The thing is there is a temptation when discussing the euro to resort to crude national stereotypes to explain what's gone wrong. But we must resist, because **it's much more complicated than that.**

It's much more complicated than:

✗ . . . the fact that **the Germans** want to rule the world, and in order to do that they make really good stuff that people actually want to buy, and then sell it on at a profit, which is of course cheating. **No, it's much more complicated than that.**

It's much more complicated than:

✗ . . . the fact that the French only want to work until Thursday lunchtime, only want to work until they're fifty-two and expect everyone else to pick up the tab. **No, it's much more complicated than that.**

It's much more complicated than:

✗ . . . the fact that Italy is one gigantic money-laundering scheme.

✗ . . . the fact that the Belgians didn't have a government for a couple of years and no one noticed.

✗ . . . the fact that Polish people want to work hard; like to work hard.

✗ . . . the fact that half of Spain is asleep and the other half hasn't got a job.

✗ . . . that Greek bloke, you know the one who picked you up from the airport and drove you to the place you were staying, which was only three-quarters of a mile but he charged you eighty-five euros, and then that evening he brought you your tea with his thumb in the hummus and fag ash in the taramasalata, and he tried to have sex with your wife. **No, it's much more complicated than that.**

See? Fool proof. You will win any argument

The euro: seeing as we're on the subject

The thing about the euro that baffles me and should baffle you as sensible thinking **Common Sense** real world people is this. We've established how complex it is, how it's much more complicated than any explanation anyone can give, but how did it end up in this situation?

After all, it must have been some very smart people that set it up, it can't have been any old idiot, this is just the kind of thing intelligent people would be involved in. And because it involves a great deal of lending money and borrowing money you might expect them to have done some checks. Just some basic checks.

After all if you or I go to a bank to borrow some money what do they do? They run some checks don't they? Look at what you earn, what you owe, what your qualifications are and so on. They do some checks.

So, you'd think whoever set up the euro might have done some checks on – just to pick a name at random out of a hat – Greece.

Because if they had they'd have found out that Greece has gone bankrupt:

✗ Not once, which would be a shame but you know, it happens to everyone at some point.
✗ Not twice, which would be careless oh hahaha so very witty.
✗ Not three times, which would suggest that some people around here aren't entirely serious.
✗ Not four times, because no one would go bankrupt four times.
✗ But five times! Five times! In 1824, 1843, 1860, 1890 and 1932.
✗ And not only that the last time Greece was in a currency union, the Latin Monetary Union, it was

kicked out in 1908* for borrowing too much money and fiddling the books. **You'd think someone might have checked.**

But no, you say, **it's much more complicated than that.**

'Who watches who's watching the people watching the watchmen?'

* They got let back in in 1910. Moral: no one ever learns.

I have a good old laugh pronouncing it
'Himmigrants', as though they're all
male. I'm currently going through a
divorce.

Barry Igot, 47, welder

IMMIGRATION

OK, well, this is the **elephant in the room**, isn't it?

And what an elephant. An Indian, African, European, the odd South American elephant in the room. Because like it or not, the fact that Europe and the EU is a giant vampire superstate hell-bent on teleporting the very milk out of British nursing mothers' bosoms and then pouring it down a drain somewhere near Dessau in eastern Germany doesn't really seem to bother anyone, no matter how horrific.

Ever since the floodgates were opened by the Tony Blair government we have been flooded by a flood of immigration. Literally. Just look at Somerset last year, flooded. Now this flooding was not caused by gay marriage as some have alleged – no, no one can cry that much – or by the shocking surprise winter weather during winter, no, this was caused by the **sheer weight of Romanian people** turning up early for the apple harvest, which caused the county to sink into the Bristol Channel. So, it is time to take action.

You can't say anything any more

So immigration is the issue of the moment. No one can deny it, even in places where there is no immigration at all, it's driving people mad, they're angry and they won't take it any more. It's undermining our way of life! Do we really want to spend all our time complaining about this when what we really want to do is whine about the weather? It's embarrassing, too. All these people coming over here working harder than us and making us look like a bunch of work-shy, entitled, soft-handed asthmatic twats.

And you could see the whole thing as a terrible comedown – they used to come over here and take our jobs, now they take our benefits. It's enough to make a grown man weep, if you were the sort of person who cried, which I most definitely am not.

But I digress. The rule of **if you don't like it here then you can fuck off** is an excellent one, but if we are going to stick with a cornerstone of British culture, fair play, the straight bat, the simple business of people being treated the same, then **it should apply to everyone**.

Trouble is, fuck off to where? Long gone are the days where you could fuck off to Australia and they'd let you in for a tenner. It's unlikely that Europe itself would be

'Because if you don't like it here go live somewhere else should apply to everyone'

all that keen on the Brits who don't like it here fucking off there, there's enough of those fat perma-tanned wankers* in Spain to drag the Spanish economy down forever.†

So: why are people coming over here? What's the attraction?

People magnet

Because there's no doubt that the UK is a person magnet. They're coming here like iron filings to a

*You leave this country to live somewhere else for whatever reason, you are dead to me.
†Then again if you are somehow making Spain worse, respect.

magnet, like flies on shit. That's come out wrong. Enticed by the lure of some of the highest wages in the world and a health service that works (and provides jobs), who can blame these people? In other words, the reason they're all coming over here is because this is the greatest country in the world. **One way to stop them coming is for a government to make things a lot worse. Look no further.**

The other is to give off a different impression to the rest of the world – in other words, try to throw the world off the scent either by somehow putting the whole of the UK in a cloaking device, like the Romulans use in *Star Trek: The Next Generation* to sneak up on Captain Picard, or to broadcast propaganda that will shatter once and for all the idea that the UK is somewhere anyone would want to come and live and work in. Seeing as the cloaking device isn't due to come online until the twenty-fifth century we will have to work with what we've got in front of us.

As it happens, we already have the means at our disposal. TV can help, in fact it's time for the BBC to pull its skirts up and remember what the B stands for. The first B. Too long the BBC has bent itself double to the EU, spreading EU Leninist Marxist propaganda like *Homes Under the Hammer* (sell off your possessions, Communist nonsense) and *Great British Bake Off* (don't be fooled, no true British person has ever really cared about cake that much, it's straight from some Brussels think-tank with full backing from the European Sponge Commission).

On that bombshell

And not only that, the BBC has been complicit in making the world think that the UK is full of great people you'd like to hang around with, who have an irreverent sense of humour, don't take themselves too seriously, yet have a deep understanding of the important things in life as well as lightly worn expertise. Friendly, bluff, well off, witty, down to earth. That's what the world thinks of us, and it's all because of *Top Gear*.

That's right: *Top Gear*. *Top Gear* is the reason the UK is held in such high esteem all over the world. Jeremy, James and l'il Richard Hammond come across as such top blokes, likeable, affable and charming, showing the true values of Britishness that we hold dear. By sheer coincidence *Top Gear* is the BBC's biggest selling programme abroad, it's sold all over the globe to something like 212 countries out of a total of 195 nation states. As a result most of the world and probably a fair chunk of outer space thinks we are all, each and every one of us, bloody great blokes.

Our finest export

All over the world Jezza, Captain Slow and The Hamster are held in high esteem. From Poland to Chile, from the

Russian Steppes to the jungles of Borneo, from the blistering hot shacks of outback Australia to the sub-zero conditions of Svalbard, from the mud huts of the Serengeti to the igloos of frozen Arctic wastes their happy-go-lucky adventures are lapped up enthusiastically. Who wouldn't want to come to the UK? Where everyone gets a new car every week, a car you can destroy without caring, and everyone is laughing all the time, and even though they are at the mercy of capricious producers the boys keep on smiling. *Top Gear* is our greatest cultural export, a more powerful ambassador than our man in Moscow, broadcasting the message that the UK is a land of top bloody blokes.

Now, I've met all three of the *Top Gear* boys and three nicer fellas you couldn't hope to meet. They really are some of the nicest geezers you'd ever make the acquaintance of. And I'm sure right now they'd be horrified to realize that it's their easy, affable charm that has brought our country to its knees, that their earnest and excellent work showing the world how we do have the Greatest Sense of Humour in the World, and that everyone is affable if somewhat clumsy and bad at map-reading and off-roading, has led us to the brink.

This is why one of the very first things a **Common Sense** revolution would do is cancel *Top Gear*.

Yes. Cancel *Top Gear*.

It pains me to say this, it really does, and what is bitter about this decision is all those humourless leftie bores who will be delighted. But we'd be cancelling it precisely because it is brilliant, funny, entertaining and all those things that certain people can't stand. It's just that its message, that the British are bloody good blokes, is simply too dangerous. There will be knighthoods and Guv'norment positions for the three *Top Gear* boys, but I'm afraid there are bigger things at stake. We need to stop the flood of people who want to come to the UK and stand around in a hangar and watch Richard Hammond tread on his own punchlines.

Phase Two

So, that's Phase One. Phase Two of what the BBC can do is this. If we want to put people off the UK they have the perfect weapon: *EastEnders*. *EastEnders* would work as a powerful repellent – anyone watching the ongoing unceasing misery of everyday EastEnd folk would never want to come to the UK. The endless love triangles, confrontations, unsolved murders and unresolved family disputes, even just the soul-sapping, heart-shuddering sight of Ian Beale's face alone would deliver a firm message that the UK is not the place to come to, let alone be trifled with.

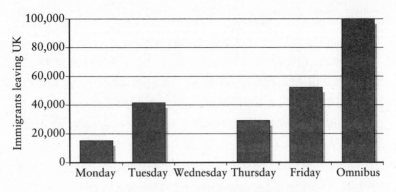

The EastEnders *Misery Theory*

So to reiterate:

- ✗ Cancel *Top Gear*. I don't want to but this is a National Emergency. It's for everyone's good;
- ✗ Beam *EastEnders* on all TV frequencies all over the world instead. In fact project Ian Beale's face on to the moon and leave it up there until the UN agrees that no one should move anywhere.

That should cancel out the UK's powerful magnetism for immigrant folk and it would have an immediate effect. And cancelling *Top Gear* would get some of the humourless hair-shirt lefties on board in case we need a national coalition.

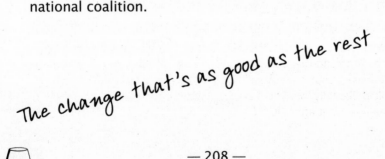

The change that's as good as the rest

Direct action

But we will need to do more.

- ✗ All British beaches to be mined. Sorry, Lady Di, this is important.
- ✗ Electrify the English Channel. Leave plugged-in bar heaters, toasters in the water.
- ✗ Brick up the Channel Tunnel, using British bricks of course. We will probably need to use Polish builders to get it done, though.
- ✗ Use the budget airline model – all major UK airports to be 500 miles from their named destination. People seeking to visit London end up in places like Lerwick or Newquay.
- ✗ A cap on the free movement of depressing Scandinavian police dramas.
- ✗ Restrictions on those wishing to enter the UK – specifically my ex, and so-called business partners who claim I still owe them money.
- ✗ Stop talking English so people who've come over here having learned English realize they've wasted their time and go home.*
- ✗ British citizens on birth to be issued with a secret password to prove they are British.

*The Welsh and the Jocks have spent huge amounts of money on not that many people speaking other languages and for a long time it looked like folly, but you have to admit that there might have been something in it after all.

✗ Passports to be replaced with a tattooed-on ID document.

✗ Clearly, one of the things luring people from abroad here is the wide range of food on offer. Restaurants to be scaled back to just serving British grub, curries etc, **Common Sense**.

If we are to take our country back we are going to have to be prepared to go the extra mile. Not the extra 1.6 kilometres. So we propose further measures.

Taking care of those who were here first

When you see the daily injustice of people who weren't here first jumping the queue of life, when you see the rights of those who should have their fair share before anyone else, any Johnny-Foreigner-come-lately, it upsets us. Maybe I'm a sensitive soul, but too bad.

And it happens all day, every day, in all sorts of ways. I think we all agree that what we all want is to protect the rights of the people who *were* here first. Enough's enough. Time to take this seriously, even though some of the Human Rights industry might say that that's unfair, that human beings are all equal; well, I say that can only go so far when faced with a group of people so hugely disadvantaged.

That is why we in **FUKP** think it is only right and proper that Ginger People, our Gingerigines if you will, should be respected, preserved and protected.

The butt of too many jokes, of easy jibes, of playground nonsense as well as disadvantaged in the sunbathing arena, the fact remains that Ginger people were here first. Before the blonds, the brunettes, the mousy people and the bald there were the Gingerigines. None of the mainstream parties, and definitely not the Greens are prepared to do what they have to do to make sure that the rights of our indigenous peoples are preserved. There are days where I feel like **Common Sense** has made me into the only sane man in a world of madmen. Or the other way round. Not sure.

So, to honour our indigenous people a new dawn will dawn:

- ✘ Prince Harry to be elevated to a new role as King of the Gingers, Danny Alexander as first minister. Their people will need leadership and Harry and Danny will be ideal.
- ✘ The Isle of Wight with its matching squirrels to be made the Ginger Kingdom, or Gingedom, the Isle of Red, Rufusisle, we'll figure out a name, Gingerstan maybe.
- ✘ Gingerigines to be recognized as a protected species; Ginger reservations with casinos to be set up.

This **Common Sense** approach to Immigration and Nationality is a complete departure from the other parties: I fully expect to see this stuff at party conferences by the end of the year with them all acting like it was their idea. Only **FUKP** has diagnosed the cause of the problem, the action that needs to be taken, then how to further extend the protection of our own people.

The protest protest party

DIPLOMACY

Working alongside our foreign friends (foreigners)

It's very important that Britain embraces the philosophy of the global village – after all, the world is smaller than it's ever been and much can be gained from sharing knowledge and information, while experiencing the many rich and diverse cultures. Except France.*
Be reasonable.

There are those who point the finger and tell me I have an island mentality. This simply isn't true. I've been on literally dozens of booze cruises to Calais, four package holidays to Turkey, not to mention a stag fortnight in Tallinn. Strictly speaking, I never really got to see much of Turkey as your drinks and booze were free if you stayed in the compound – a bit like a G4 summit, except it wasn't Angela Merkel hogging the sunbeds, but a group of her fellow countrymen. Nice fellas, though touchy about the war for some reason. I suppose I wouldn't want reminding either.

*If it is a global village then that means someone must be the global village idiot. I'll leave that one to you.

So never let it be said that I haven't experienced foreign climes. I also have plenty of experience when it comes to dealing with foreign officials – delicate negotiations with superpowers and heads of state are nothing compared to negotiating the release of fifteen pissed-up scaffolders from an Estonian nick. Often I think if instead of fancy ambassadors we had ordinary fellas maybe supping a couple of pints together rather than la-di-da diplomat types the paranoia and hostility that led to the First World War would have been avoided. 'Knock it off Fritz, you're out of order, mate.' 'Entschuldigen, you are right, Tommy. Pint?'

Of course, we can't talk about foreign policy without mentioning the 'Special Relationship', and no I'm not talking about the agreement I have with the brewery on soon to be out-of-date beer. I speak of the 'Special Relationship' with our American cousins.

I'm only too aware that there are those who think that Britain spends far too much time brown-nosing the US government. Personally speaking, I'm not too keen on the photo opportunity every President has in an Irish boozer. One sip of Guinness and he's on his toes. Now if he were to visit my gaff, protocol would suggest that he'd have to down his pint in one, stay 'til closing time and have a game of killer pool during the lock-in, in order to put the seal on our proud nations' solidarity. At the moment the 'Special Relationship' seems to involve us buying them dinner and then them doing us up the bum.

There are those people who might say to me, 'Guv, can we really trust you to represent us and speak up for our best interests?' Put it like this – if I was sat in the United Nations, and someone had slagged off the pound or had a go at our pub grub, I'd have no hesitation in getting to my feet and start banging my pint glass on the desk and telling them to wind their neck in, like that Russian chess player did all those years ago.

Summit opening gambits

International summits, the G7, G8 whatever, I can't keep up. These giant helicopter-studded events serve two purposes. They're a chance for all the world's leaders to get together and have their photo taken, a photo that can then be pored over by the *Have I Got News For You* team in search of a funny line. They also offer a chance to turn the water cannon on the niffy anti-globalization types who turn up to protest. Everyone's happy. But these occasions are all about first impressions, leadership, and getting good headlines at home.

Anyway, here are some **Common Sense** approaches to foreign leaders:

Barack Obama: 'How about you make your mind up for once, pal?'
Vladimir Putin: 'Do one.'
Angela Merkel: 'Watch it. You've been too quiet

for too long . . . yes, you know exactly what I mean, Ange.'

François Hollande: 'Who are you again?'

The Italian PM: 'Where's Silvio? He seems like a laugh.'

Head of the EU: Here's your chance to spin on your heels and make a dramatic exit while crying, 'Good day to you, sir!'

Head of the IMF, wassername: 'What do you know, love?'

These direct approaches will mean you won't get invited to too many of these time-wasting international summits and you can get on with the more important business of domestic politics. **Common Sense**.

Vladimir Putin can do one

DEFENCE

He who defends everything defends nothing. Frederick the Great

If ever there was a country the whole world looks to for the right way to go in defence it's the UK. Undisputed World War Champions of the World, we have also dealt with different trouble zones all over the world over the last hundred years or so as we withdrew from them.

However, the world is changing and the various threats out there are changing too.

A changing world

When previously what we used to do was slug it out victoriously with our near neighbours, or send some boats around the world to enforce our will, we now have the threat of terror and people in far-off lands plotting to do terrible things to us. The world is changing. The technology is changing. The enemy is changing.

It has been heartening in recent months to see the RAF back in action. Personally, I think the time for empty gestures in dealing with the likes of ISIS has ended and we need to do something serious about it – I'd send the Red Arrows as soon as possible over to Iraq so that they can sky-write 'KNOCK IT OFF YOU CUNTS' and let those mental murderous bastards know that we are not to be trifled with.

Thing is, these new enemies are something we have to get to grips with doing something about. Can these people be reasoned with? Are they even acting rationally? Some of them have fled places like Leicester and Crawley, so they're not completely out of their minds. But what can we possibly offer these grim beheading bastards? Probably the very best laser-guided munitions money can buy. In fact, I think anyone in the top tax bracket should be allowed to Tippex a personal message or greeting onto every Paveway missile sent out to the Middle East. It'd take the edge off the government having half of what you earn, I'd expect.

So while we're looking at this ISIS thing the powers that be seem to think that drone warfare seems to be the way to go. Now, this of course means our boys and girls don't end up in danger, and that is a good thing no doubt, but for all that – Think It Through: it does mean that war documentaries are going to stink to high heaven in the future. You can't interview the robot, and the ageing nerd who flew it from a Portakabin outside Daventry is hardly going to give you a misty-eyed look as he describes going into battle and blatting a school or a wedding by accident. It's not exactly *The World at War*, is it?

Punching above your weight

Our forces are the best in the world, of course, which must be why modern politicians seem to believe that even if they reduce the army to eleven blokes and a khaki forklift we will continue to punch above our weight. This has to stop. The world needs to tremble in fear at the merest mention of the UK's armed forces and six sappers with one high-tech shovel between them isn't how to do it.

So, we need to take radical action. As usual. I seem to be spending most of this book urging radical action. But this is modern politics; I'm hardly going to say leave well alone, am I?

There are some simple points that need making:

✗ Germany has been too quiet for too long. Just sayin'.
✗ Sharing an aircraft carrier with France simply won't work. We'd have to sink it the day we gave it back to them. Has no one Thought This Through? Bloody Gordon Brown.
✗ If Russia is going to kick off again Chelsea will have to be impounded as an enemy asset and busted up for scrap. It's an ill wind etc.

✘ Health and Safety culture has turned the modern battlefield into a Health and Safety nightmare: 'Bayonets are dangerous things and should not be fixed at any point.' It's a joke.

✘ Who invited the lawyers?

Proud tradition

Like any lad brought up properly in the UK I am aware that this country has great resources at its disposal. The Welsh, for instance, who as the film *Zulu* tells us, when backed into a corner and/or surrounded will take down every last living bastard with them. The Scots also, whose worldwide reputation is as fearless warriors, prepared to fight to the last man for a plateful of lambs' innards or an inevitable poor result in an international football fixture. And the English, whose mastery of all forms of warfare is largely down to the centuries of practice offered to them by the Welsh, the Scots and of course the Irish, who when short of someone to fight, fight themselves.

We once had the biggest navy in the world, and one that was politically correct years before anyone had heard of the concept: a one-eyed one-armed admiral in charge, and not just tokenism either, he was winning battles long before Brent Council insisted on that kind of thing. Our air force showed the world the way in the Battle of Britain, when, without really making the effort, we chased the Luftwaffe off in Spitfires and Hurricanes with cups of tea in the cockpit while the British public carried on business as usual style. Etc. You get the picture. You know this stuff. Glenn Miller. Vera Lynn. We stood alone. I don't need to remind you, even if some of the younger kids have no idea.

So what are we to do with this proud tradition, and how are we to address it to our modern world, as well as learning the lesson of the last couple of decades that anything Tony Blair tells you has to be taken with a skip load of salt?

No plan survives contact with the enemy

Here are some defence talking points that I think might help us bridge our proud traditions and the challenges of the future:

- ✗ Immediate recommencing of the Hundred Years War, try to get it up to Two Hundred Years.
- ✗ The UK to undertake a moon-shot – to prepare first line of defence against actual aliens – no other party is offering this anywhere in the world, it would show we were leading the way and provide the edge for British technological innovation. In a patriotic echo of the Battle of Britain, people will have to hand in their non-stick frying pans to help to build the heat-shield needed for the capsule.

- ✗ NATO to have a good, long hard think about whether having both Greece and Turkey in it is at all sensible, and whether the great alliance isn't storing up a ton of trouble for itself.
- ✗ National Service, but only for people who don't want to do it.
- ✗ To do what we can to protect the Falklands we will strengthen the garrison in Gibraltar.
- ✗ Order four more squadrons of Spitfires, reopen Biggin Hill, Manston and Duxford. These squadrons can patrol the Channel looking for Romanian boat people.
- ✗ Replace medium-range nuclear missiles with free-range nuclear missiles – never let it be said I'm not Green.
- ✗ UK terror threat levels to be binned as part of my crackdown on Health and Safety nonsense – a new level of **Don't Panic for Christ's sake, we're British** to be brought in.
- ✗ Students to get free education if they go into the army. OK, is that a deal, kids?
- ✗ An end to costly foreign wars: the UK will simply issue a UN resolution entitled **'Come and Have a Go if You Think You're Hard Enough'** and that should save us the bother of having to fly all our stuff in and out.
- ✗ As a result of scything cuts by previous administrations, the RAF's capabilities will be limited to photobombing.
- ✗ Invade Syria – this time without soldiers (we haven't

got enough and it might contravene Health and Safety law).

✗ A series of inquiries will be commissioned into why all military inquiries take so long.

✗ A common enemy of the state to be appointed by committee. Only shifty-looking non-English speakers will be considered for this role.

✗ All chemical weapons to be scrapped and replaced by Periodical Table weapons.

And finally:

✗ The Afghan War (our Fourth or Fifth, I forget which) is drawing to an end and thank God for that. One thing to remember is that our boys and girls have been out there for thirteen years, three years longer than the Russian involvement in the country, which is great because it doesn't mean we look like poofs on the international stage. But I will be the first to admit that it's not always gone according to plan, that our aims have been confused, some of our kit not up to scratch, our politicians not entirely honest. But enough mithering, what do we do? Well, I think we can make amends for some of this, for the way we have fought this war with one hand behind our back and one foot on the door, like a snooker trick shot you know you're going to muff. We've flown our stuff in and out and it's hampered how effective we have been able to be. So, to make up for this I think the British Army instead of flying its stuff out should pack its gear up and fight its way back to the UK. Head west, out through Afghanistan, into Iran, give them a good kicking, take out their nuke gear; into Iraq, again – 'Remember us?' and sort ISIS out good and proper; into Syria and hand Assad his arse on a plate; into Turkey to teach them a lesson they won't forget; into Bulgaria – never had a war with them, might be a giggle; up into Poland, smash the place up, then their builders will have to go home to fix it up (joined-up thinking); a victory lap through Germany – I did say they've been too quiet too long; down through Holland and Belgium and back out through the Channel Tunnel. Jackpot. Operation Xenophon.

Some of this might seem tough, but when the going gets tough, this country ain't afraid of no one or nothing. All right? Did you spill my pint?

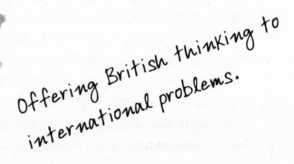

Offering British thinking to international problems.

GREAT BRITONS

NO. 17: PIERS MORGAN

Before reality TV and those magazines which talk about soap operas as though they're real life, Britain was a very dull place. As forbidding and downcast as an *EastEnders* omnibus, the nation was utterly grey and devoid of any personality whatsoever – a bit like Gary Lineker before he had any writers.

Britain was holding out for a hero, someone to drag it out of the drab corner it had painted itself into. And so, as they say, cometh the hour, cometh the man. Piers Morgan, a bright, spunky young thing, was dragged from obscurity by Kelvin MacKenzie, the then editor of the *Sun*, to edit the newspaper's dirty phone-line ads. His only words of advice to the young Morgan were to 'make sure there are no minge hairs showing in the pictures of the dolly birds and put Arthur Scargill's home number in there for a laugh'. From there Morgan went on to edit the paper's Bizarre page, sealing legendary status in the tabloid pantheon by running a story about how Dirty Den had sprained an ankle, but was now on the mend.

As a result of Morgan's ability to sniff out a good story concerning Samantha Fox's dislike for foreign food, or Simon Le Bon's inability to shed those extra pounds, he was always going to be headhunted by people whose job it is to hunt for people's heads.

Wind forward a few years to a particularly low point in Morgan's career. Sadly for Piers, he was fired from his dream job of giving editorial approval for the publication of faked photographs featuring British soldiers breaking the Geneva Convention. It seemed like he'd reached the end of the road – indeed, so far down the road had he gone, he was literally left tilting helplessly over the edge – just like that bit (SPOILERS) at the end of *The Italian Job* where they failed to get away with the gold.

However, just when he'd reached his lowest ebb (which strangely enough coincided with a national feeling of euphoria) Morgan's luck changed. He was given his first big chance to shine on television as a judge on *Britain's Got Talent*. His catchphrase 'That's not very good' was soon sweeping the nation. Indeed, such was Piers's popularity that Simon Cowell dispatched him off to America, where he became a judge on *America's Got Talent*. The same show, except it had 'America' in front, instead of 'Britain'.

In the US he was given his own chat show, *Piers Morgan Live*, in which he met people even more important than himself. He also used the show as a platform to tell his American audience that firearms are dangerous and should only be handled by experts such as soldiers, policemen, and lone gunmen.

His television success continued in the UK with his series *Piers Morgan's Life Stories*, in which he met people who had life stories. In one of the show's most renowned exchanges he asked Cilla Black, 'Have you got a book coming out on 11 March?' to which she replied, 'Yes, and I'll be signing copies in the Walsall branch of Waterstones from 2 p.m. onwards tomorrow.'

Piers has etched himself into the nation's heart, like one of those bugs that swims up your urine and then burrows its way out of your bladder, through your guts, up past your lungs and into your left ventricle. His breezy expertise on all matters, especially sporting, always garners a hearty response on social media, where other tweeters seem keen to find new ways to spell 'areshole' and 'fucker'. Without a doubt a national treasure he will be sorely missed when ███████ ████████████████ ████████████ ██████████nl███████████████████s ███████ ████████████████████

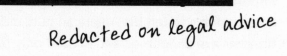

Redacted on legal advice

POINT OF VIEW

Is it really so wrong to be spacist?

Right, well it's time for us to talk about this. Various members of **FUKP** over the years have said things about people from outer space that have been taken out of context, misrepresented and used to smear us, drag our good name through the mud.

Well, **FUKP** is not a spacist party. Let me make that clear right now. Indeed, if anyone was to ask me about aliens and outer space, they'd find that I have spoken to plenty of aliens, that my understanding of cultures across the galaxy is at least as good as anyone else's, and that the inference that I might be spacist myself is outrageous, and does not get any less outrageous with repetition.

For instance: only last night I enjoyed a long chat with a Q't-arl from the Figel Cluster. I forget his name, I called him Quincy because his Q't-arl name is unpronounceable in English. I will confess that I find Quincy entirely repulsive to behold, that his culture and its traditions are literally alien to me, and the thought of my daughter bringing a Q't-arl home to meet her parents is completely disgusting, but I am not in any way spacist, and in fact enjoy Figel takeaway food. I will admit that in the past former **FUKP** treasurer Steve referred to one of our Q't-arl friends as a 'dirty, stinking, paedo Q-ball', a term entirely offensive to inhabitants of the Figel system, but he was on painkillers, tired, had been drinking and thought no one was listening, let alone filming it on their iPhone. He won't do it again, at least not while his back is better.

While some of my best friends are not aliens, I have been photographed with many alien people on many occasions. I have not smiled in any of these pictures not, as has been suggested, because I am spacist, but because a human smile could possibly offend alien peoples not familiar with Earth emotions. And often, when wearing their face-covering atmospheric masks their own alien emotions are impossible to ascertain: I would not presume to smile when I don't know if they are smiling back or not.

I reiterate: **FUKP** is not a spacist party. But we are clear that should any Venusians seek asylum, regardless of how hot the surface of their planet might be, we would not welcome them. Not because we don't like the smell of the nitrous atmosphere they require for sustenance, nor because their ritual mating and spawning habits are disturbingly arousing, but because pressure on council housing has the system at breaking point. That Venusians are able to recycle their effluent into agricultural fertilizer 150 per cent more efficient

THE PUB LANDLORD

PUTTING
SLOGANS FIRST

Vote for the Free United Kingdom Party

Paging Ed Miliband.

**NEW BRITAIN
NEW VISION
NEW CONTACT LENSES**

"LET'S GO
BACKWARD
TOGETHER"

6 stages of forcing your noble Remembrance Face

1. Oh no, I'm at the Cenotaph and hungover.

2. Quick! Think sad thoughts.

3. That's it: when the dog died.

4. Too sad.

5. Keep it together, man! Never cry in public.

6. Perfectly noble.

than any Terran fertilizer is not the point. They are not welcome here. There, I've said it. I don't want one moving in next door.

Now, the truth is in fact that we in **FUKP** are the only people unafraid to stand up to the whole Space Relations industry, an insidious organization and movement who will stop at nothing to stifle the free expression of the ordinary people of this country who, it so happens, simply cannot cope with the thought of aliens amongst them. Not because they are from space, but because they are taking up ours. We are a tolerant people, with a proud history of respect for other cultures, but we find that the naturally intolerant culture of, for instance, the Paahn Folk from the Paahn Planet, who demand that we respect their ancient gods even though they look exactly the same as Peppa Pig almost impossible to accommodate. The truth hurts, but if

'Not in my beer garden'

Peppa, George, Mummy Pig and Daddy Pig offend you so much, maybe the ammonia-fields in the Rings of Paahn where you came from is where you actually belong. But I digress.

These accusations of spacism tarnish everyone, the accuser and the accused. The merest allegation of spacism is enough to shut down conversation, is used to stifle debate, often exploited as a deliberate misunderstanding to close down what people really want to say. When, for instance, I say that it makes me feel sick to the stomach when I see that the BBC news is being read by a DjoMurian She-He, it is not because I am spacist but because I wish the job had gone to someone from this planet. Yet again, the BBC letting down the people whose money is extorted from them to pursue a galactic agenda that is not in their interests.

This shutting down of honest debate cannot continue. For as long as we are facing this influx of Paahn, Q't-arl, Venusian, Nuvian Mecha-Men, Ttelracs, Wolliwyam and the other billions of life forms that the Blair/Brown government flung the doors open to and welcomed with open arms, issues of exactly how aliens fit into the UK will go on to cause trouble for future generations.

MULTICULTURALI-SM

Pass the Duchy of Cornwall by the left-hand side. Sonic Youth

Uh oh. Here we go. Into the rapids we go. The Shit Creek Rapids that lead direct to Turd Lagoon via Haemorrhoid Rocks. Explaining Economics? A doddle. Sorting out democracy? Convincing Vince Cable to give someone a 'shout-out' on Question Time? Couldn't be simpler.

But multiculturalism. **Bloody hell.** It's where Anglo-Saxons fear to tread.

Multiculturalism is what, Guv? I'm glad you asked me that question. Well, it's all about live and let live. It's all about getting people from different places to live alongside one another and get along. And you do that by everyone respecting everyone else's way of life. Sort of.

In other words, what with human nature, culture and what bloody-minded bastards people can be and are, it's the impossible dream. It's a punch-up waiting to happen, it's a potential powder keg and someone at some point is going to get their fingers burned by that powder keg, and will subsequently be forced to run their fingers under a cold tap for ten minutes.

People up and down the land are upset about it, about where it leads us, because it's another Bright Idea.

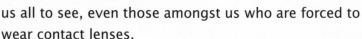

The warning signs indicate that multiculturalism's time is up. Because it's got too big for its boots, and has outstayed its welcome. The signs are there for us all to see, even those amongst us who are forced to wear contact lenses.

One of the things that is definitely happening up and down the land is that Christmas is under threat. Under attack. Yes. From multiculturalism. And you can tell Christmas is under attack because it has swollen up like an allergic reaction or a puffer fish chucking out its spikes in self-defence. This is why year on year Christmas gets bigger and bigger, in a desperate attempt to fight off the threat from Diwali and Hanukkah and the other ones I've not heard of. All of those Christmas TV specials which are set at Christmas and bang on about it being Christmas are a direct result of Christmas being under attack. Those carols, the Christmas music you hear in the supermarket in early

November – these are the battle hymns of the resistance.

So: in other words, when you see Christmas decorations for sale in late August, you know who is to blame. You know. I don't need to say. And there's atheists, the heathen bastards, who if they could, would cancel Christmas and bin it right off. If they had their way they'd put Santa on show trial, shoot the sorry mythical bastard, make his elves redundant and employ a vet to destroy his reindeer. This is why Christmas gets bigger and bigger and starts earlier and earlier every year: it's defending itself from being relentlessly undermined. And that's just not British. Proper Christmas starts at 4 p.m. on Christmas Eve, and ends Boxing Day evening when you get home with a bargain sofa that you realize you haven't got room for.

Having studied this all at great length and detail, I can safely say that where it's all gone tits up (to paraphrase Dr King) is this whole, sorry business of being offended on someone else's behalf. Local councils have entire departments who devote most of their time being offended on behalf of various races and religions. It's their job to decide that Mr Chaudry is very aggrieved by his neighbour, Mr Taylor's, Christmas tree, in spite of the fact Mr Chaudry is more perplexed by that wombat Mr Cartwright, whose gaff is covered with 227,000 fairy lights flashing on and off, 24/7, than he is by a

'There's extreme, extremer and extremist. It's not a competition.'

six-foot conifer with some baubles and a fairy sat on the top.

The thing is, this whole thing they labelled 'multiculturalism' sprung up out of nowhere when politicians decided they had to figure out how to get people to live alongside one another in harmony. So with this in mind, it's little wonder it's gone wrong. Because it was invented by politicians it got tangled up things like . . . er, vote-winning. And once votes are involved you do what you can not to piss people off, so you start turning a blind eye, you worry about what and what not to say. In other words, you don't stand up and say, 'Oi, that's bang out of order!' especially not if it's people you think might be voting for you. Even when they're raping people and stuff. Hmmm.

Multiculturalism Timeline

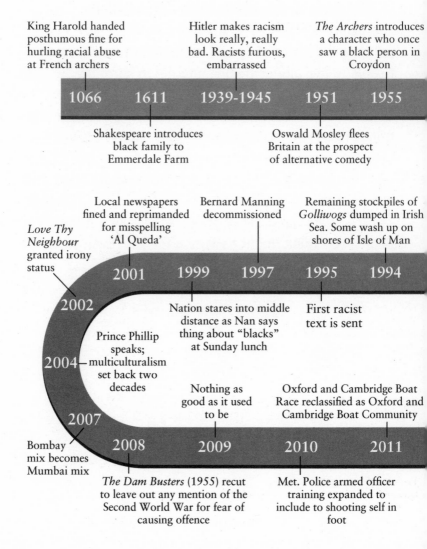

King Harold handed posthumous fine for hurling racial abuse at French archers

Hitler makes racism look really, really bad. Racists furious, embarrassed

The Archers introduces a character who once saw a black person in Croydon

1066   1611   1939-1945   1951   1955

Shakespeare introduces black family to Emmerdale Farm

Oswald Mosley flees Britain at the prospect of alternative comedy

Love Thy Neighbour granted irony status

Local newspapers fined and reprimanded for misspelling 'Al Queda'

Bernard Manning decommissioned

Remaining stockpiles of *Golliwogs* dumped in Irish Sea. Some wash up on shores of Isle of Man

2001   1999   1997   1995   1994

2002

Nation stares into middle distance as Nan says thing about "blacks" at Sunday lunch

First racist text is sent

2004 — Prince Phillip speaks; multiculturalism set back two decades

Nothing as good as it used to be

Oxford and Cambridge Boat Race reclassified as Oxford and Cambridge Boat Community

2007

Bombay mix becomes Mumbai mix

2008   2009   2010   2011

The Dam Busters (1955) recut to leave out any mention of the Second World War for fear of causing offence

Met. Police armed officer training expanded to include to shooting self in foot

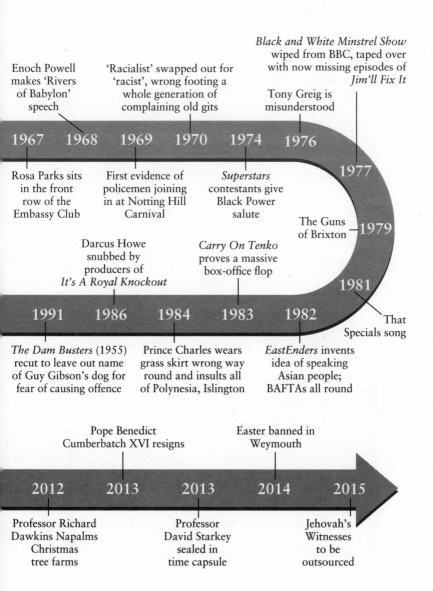

Enoch Powell makes 'Rivers of Babylon' speech

'Racialist' swapped out for 'racist', wrong footing a whole generation of complaining old gits

Black and White Minstrel Show wiped from BBC, taped over with now missing episodes of *Jim'll Fix It*

Tony Greig is misunderstood

1967 1968 1969 1970 1974 1976

1977

Rosa Parks sits in the front row of the Embassy Club

First evidence of policemen joining in at Notting Hill Carnival

Superstars contestants give Black Power salute

The Guns of Brixton

1979

Darcus Howe snubbed by producers of *It's A Royal Knockout*

Carry On Tenko proves a massive box-office flop

1981

1991 1986 1984 1983 1982

That Specials song

The Dam Busters (1955) recut to leave out name of Guy Gibson's dog for fear of causing offence

Prince Charles wears grass skirt wrong way round and insults all of Polynesia, Islington

EastEnders invents idea of speaking Asian people; BAFTAs all round

Pope Benedict Cumberbatch XVI resigns

Easter banned in Weymouth

2012 2013 2013 2014 2015

Professor Richard Dawkins Napalms Christmas tree farms

Professor David Starkey sealed in time capsule

Jehovah's Witnesses to be outsourced

— 239 —

We all know what's caused the problems in the NHS but if I tell you what I think they'll lock me up for inciting racial hatred.

Carl Spitford, 25, regional organizer for Milton Keynes Against Terroristsism (MKAT)

LIFE IS UNFAIR

The elites and how they are right now laughing at you from their ivory towers right now

Life is unfair. Everyone knows that. In fact I am on record as having said many times that life is 'a series of endless, relentless, grinding disappointments'. And I know, having spoken to audiences up and down the country, that this is utterly true.

But life is unfair because the dice are loaded.

For instance, the law. The law is in the hands of a group of people who, simply by virtue of having learned how the law works, seem to think it is up to them to practise it. The legal elite, laughing at you and me with their wigs on. These people don't know the first thing about actual justice. Yet they stand between you and me and justice and the fucking nonsense that is having to clean a deep-fat fryer regularly for some reason; none of those people who ate those Kievs died. Laughing at you from their ivory tower thinking you're idiots.

And then there's the medical profession. Telling us what the science is. Well, shut it. I know my body better than anyone else. And anyway they're just doing what the drug companies tell them with their massive amounts of money spent on research to recoup, the bastards. Seven years at medical school is no substitute for having a good old jangle of my nuts, a cough and couple of aspirin, whatever is wrong with me. Maybe pop on an extra vest to sweat it out. Vaccines are actually marked POISON, right up until they get the syringe out, everyone knows that, because they contain diseases and sewage. Every doctor who says to you, 'No I can't give you antibiotics, it's a cold,' is laughing at you from his ivory tower and thinks you are an idiot. Though I will say I agree with the whole homeopathy is bollocks thing: watered-down beer, no matter how powerful the placebo effect, doesn't work. End of.

And then there's the evolution lot. Old Dickie Dawkins. Knock it off, pal. Anyone whose best friend is a mollusc isn't worth your time of day. And we get it, mate, you don't believe in God. I don't believe in fairies but do you hear me banging on about it all day long? No. Why? Because when I became a man I gave up childish things. And besides, evolution is a nonsense. Easy to disprove: if evolution is true, and we evolved from chimps, why are there still chimps? Yet there he is, sneering at us, laughing at us from his ivory tower thinking we are all idiots.

Who do these people think they are? Who put them in charge? What gives them the divine right to carry on like this? Don't they know that we, the people, know better?

What can we do to kick back against the elites, apart from get law degrees, become doctors? Well, we can go online. We can send each other emails around with stuff in that has pictures of kittens saying 'DOES THIS KITTEN NEED MMR?' We can shout, 'Bullshit, fringe boy!' each and every time Professor Brian Cox comes on the telly. And that way we will gradually pull down their ivory towers. And no longer will they be laughing at us. It might cost us a measles outbreak or two, but we must be heard. It is time.

Life is a series of endless, relentless, grinding disappointments

A vote for me is a vote

FIRST PAST THE POST

Because L is for Liberals and also for losers

OK, time for a history lesson. Now, I hope you're sitting down. Long ago, about a hundred years ago or so the Liberals – that's what they were called back then, they didn't call themselves Democratic – used to be the government. That's right. On their own, no help from anyone else.

I know.

Seriously, I'm not shitting you.

I haven't banged my head.

I haven't stood up too quickly.

I've not been at the Meow Meow.

The Liberal Party for a fair while was one of the Big Two, doing battle with the Tories, as the baton of governing this mighty country of ours got passed back and forth. And this was when the British Empire was at its height. And yes, it was the Liberals wot done it.

This is staggering stuff when you look into it. The Liberals were what young people call Badass. They took on the House of Lords to bring in National Insurance (I mean it's great that they did that but I always pay cash so you'll have to sort your own NI, mate). They built tons of enormous battleships, did a professional job of winding up the Germans and generally acted unlike Liberals. Not one mention of wind farms. No immediate root-and-branch reform of the parole system etc. No lentils, or fold-up bikes or any of these easy jibes that are also completely true. In fact none of any of that recognizable Liberal stuff.

Famous Liberals include Gladstone, who was PM four times. Four times! Eat that, Gordon Brown. Gladstone spent a great deal of his career giving the Irish the runaround. Respect.

Another big Liberal was Lloyd George, aka the Welsh Wizard, who was PM for the second half of the First World War. A monstrous shagger, Lloyd George could have sued for peace, but half the country's husbands being out of the country probably suited him down to the ground.

It may sound unlikely, but the Liberals got us into the First World War and got us out of it: all with a win as well. That's right. The Liberals. No wonder Nick Clegg looks so wistful, a hundred years ago he would have been despatching the Royal Navy off with a division of Fusiliers, a troop of Horse Guards and a Regiment of Artillery to fight the Hottentots, rather than grind his teeth at the merest mention of student loans.

'DREAMING OF HOTTENTOTS'

And the most famous Liberal of all was Winston Churchill. Churchill, who did whatever he bloody well liked and switched from the Tories when he knew they were going nowhere, became a Liberal Cabinet minister. Then he switched back to the Tories, because he did whatever he bloody well liked. It was no coincidence that he switched back to the Conservatives once the Liberals were done for.

Because what did for the Liberals was two things:

One: the arrival on the scene of the Labour Party, who, at that point, represented working people – I did ask, are you sitting down? I hope so, that one is truly astonishing.

And two: everyone getting the vote. This combination meant that all of a sudden rather than either coming first or second in an election, the Liberals started coming third.

Trouble is, they hadn't boxed clever and planned for this electoral wipeout, even though it was them that gave everyone the vote in the first place. The Liberal Party, who'd set up the pension system, hadn't made provision for their own future. They hadn't sorted out the electoral system while they had the chance and it did for them. They didn't Think It Through. The doughnuts.

FUKP
**VOTE
FOR THE
GUV'NOR**

Because of First Past the Post, the way things worked then and the way things work now means winning is everything, coming second – well, that's too bad, you never know, folks might change their mind next time, but coming third is basically crap.

First Past the Post works like this: the person who gets the most votes wins. That's it. But not the most votes in the country, oh no. The most in your local constituency. And all the others across the country. So your party can win the election and become the government even when more people have voted for the other side, just not in the right places. Now that might seem unfair, that might make you think well, the electorate are being robbed, they're being turned over, is there no justice in the world, and then the party you support wins and you think fuck it yeah, a win's a win. Tough shit the rest of you.

This is how it works. In 2005 Tony Blair tonked the Tories, smacked their arses good and proper, even though he was the most hated man on the planet in all history ever according to everyone now. Task: find someone now who'll say they voted for him. Impossible. But Blair won himself a big majority thanks to his unique electoral magic. But how many people voted for the world's most unpopular leader ever who nevertheless delivered Labour a historic third win? The numbers tell a story, and they are presented with all the reverence and respect that the electorate is due. This is how the Big Three did:

- ✗ Labour: 9,552,436 tragic, brainwashed muppets;
- ✗ Tories: 8,782,192 misguided, addled fools;
- ✗ Liberal Democrats: 5,985,454 desperate, friendless dreamers.

But what did that translate into in terms of seats in the House of Commons? Labour got 355 seats, the Conservatives got 198 seats. The Liberal Democrats got 62 seats. A travesty. Unjust. Unfair. Shabby. Undeserved. Inequitable. Unmerited. And beyond farcical. Or, if you're the Labour Party: 'Hahahahahahahaha

IN YOUR

FACE!!!!!'

Let's look at this result as two pie charts:

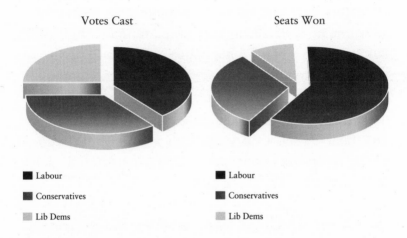

Votes Cast

Seats Won

■ Labour
■ Conservatives
▨ Lib Dems

■ Labour
■ Conservatives
▨ Lib Dems

Stone me. You can hear them laughing at you, can't you? And you can hear the Lib Dems sobbing bitter defeated tears.

If this doesn't tell you everything you need to know about how much time your average Liberal spends kicking themselves then I don't know what will. It may also go some way to explaining why even now, despite being the most despised man in the world since records began, Tony Blair has the world's greatest shit-eating grin.

Then in 2010 what happened?

✘ The Tories picked up a million votes more than Blair had in 2005, with 10,703,654 blundering eejits voting for them;

✘ Labour got about 100,000 less than in 2005 with 8,606,517 saps falling for it again;

✘ And the Lib Dems did better than ever, with 6,836,248 churls voting for them and they won five less seats!

Pies again!

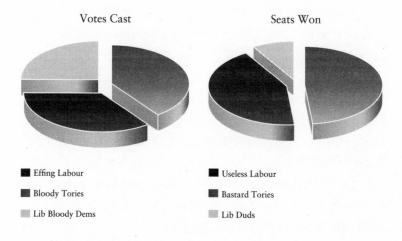

Votes Cast

- ■ Effing Labour
- ■ Bloody Tories
- ▨ Lib Bloody Dems

Seats Won

- ■ Useless Labour
- ■ Bastard Tories
- ▨ Lib Duds

As long as it suits the Big Two that's how it will stay. Every now and again the Liberals suggest changing how it works and every now and again the others consider the notion and say: 'Nah, piss off.'

And rightly so, if the odds were stacked in your or my favour like that, what would you do? Leave well alone, that's what.

Now the problem here is obvious. Eventually the people who vote for whoever comes third or below start to wonder what the point is of anything at all, which creates problems of its own, especially for the kind of parties that don't espouse a **Common Sense** approach like I do.

Because obviously they want to be different from the main parties, and they want to stand up for something different. The problem with this, of course, is that pretty quickly you end up where the Greens are, planning to stick Her Majesty in a council house* just to make people think you are cool. Grow up. She's got too much stuff to live in a council house and besides, she'd not get one for nine years as she'd be at the back of the queue. That Green policy demonstrates the true freedom of the loser. You can say what you like, no one will ever hold you to it, nothing will ever come of it, you can promise any old cack and it will never come back to bite you on the arse.

* A proper council house, I mean; not the one she lives in now.

Unless, of course, you go into coalition.

That's why we're about making promises we know you might like the sound of, but we are honest enough to say we have no intention of keeping them. Honesty in politics. The **Common Sense** response to First Past the Post.

Honestly making the Kind of promises no one could Keep

PROPOSED BANK HOLIDAY NAME CHANGES

OLD	NEW
New Year's Day	St Neurofen Day
Good Friday	Traffic Jam Friday
Easter Monday	St Cadbury's Day
May Bank Holiday	B&Q Day
Spring Bank Holiday	All-Dayer Day
Summer Bank Holiday	National Umbrella Day
Christmas Day	Gaviscon Day
Boxing Day	DFS Sofas Day

ANOTHER GREEN WORLD

'The life we could live and how the planet would prefer it', by Greg Non-Bio

Gaia, Mother Earth, has had enough. Today, here in my yurt-dwelling – fashioned by hand from ancient straw and dung I produced myself – the rain throbs on the flat roof. I have a flat roof in defiance of the convention of a roof that points arrogantly at the sky, and in order to allow the rain time to recover from its impact with my roof before it is drained in the filtering vats that drain into the earth bath.

As the roof sags I stop to consider the planet. Mother Earth is sagging. Mother Earth is tired. Mother Earth has had enough. I said that already. The virulent strain that has brought the planet to its knees is, of course, Mankind.

Mankind has done more to the planet than any other species. The Earth's poorest turn of luck and misfortune was the emergence of *Homo sapiens* over *Homo neanderthalis*. Had Mankind never evolved the planet right now would not be experiencing any of what it is going through. Mass extinctions. Not just the headline-grabbing Giant Pandas and White Tigers, or the much mourned Diplodocus but some of Creation's smaller creatures, brutally trampled by Mankind. Or should that be Man-Unkind?

Consider the Smallpox virus. This virus was minding its own business for millennia, in cows and cattle, and then Mankind appeared on the scene, enslaved the cattle against their will – and before you say anything, who can argue that cows don't have consciousness? Has anyone asked a cow? No, there is work still to be done – and the virus crossed over to humanity. Biologically hijacked and held against its will. Completely unsuitable to its new host, it did what any lifeform would do: Smallpox fought back and did everything in its power to get shot of mankind. Its reward? Biology was tricked with vaccines and Smallpox was stamped out. Eradicated. Made extinct. This example can be . . .

. . . sorry the roof is dripping onto the Amstrad, and then I had to restart the cooking-oil generator. We had falafel chips at the weekend so there's some oil but it clogs the carburettor. Where was I? Did you know that before mankind weather patterns were stable, reliable, calm? While there may be no data to go on in that there were no people to measure, quantify, cut down into slices and generally belittle what went before, what we can be certain of is that the planet would have been a calmer place. Yet now the oceans boil with storms, waves, tides.

Why? Some say the tides can be accounted for by the presence of the Moon. But for anyone to be certain of this a control experiment would be necessary, a test period of a month or maybe two without the Moon orbiting the Earth. We have other priorities and the cost of such an experiment would be prohibitive, as well as possibly damaging to the Earth's atmosphere with the rockets required to remove the Moon, and so on. Until this experiment can be carried out however, doubt remains. But what we can be sure of is that until Mankind showed up, the only thing disturbing the seas was the majestic sight of Whales and Dolphins and Flying Fish and other majestic creatures breaking the ocean's smooth and otherwise undisturbed surface. Then, Mankind, having eaten every creature in Africa apart from those animals fierce, fast or strong enough to resist Gaia's greatest mistake, set sail for new climes and species to destroy. From the first tiny coracle to the city-sized supertanker, Mankind has made waves, disrupted the seas, shattered Nature's natural patterns. And yet when one of these Man-made storms or waves comes along, does Mankind take it as a bitter reminder of where we have gone wrong?

Of course not. If only the planet could have been inoculated against Man. If only we the human race could somehow do the right thing and remove ourselves from the planet as soon as possible. When will our politicians grasp this nettle? Why is democracy dragging its heels on this issue? And this is why I have decided to change my mind and campaign in favour of nuclear power, in the sincere hope that a terrible accident will happen and remove Mankind from the face of the Earth, and give way to the Giant Upright Rabbit People, who will surely follow, hideous, usurping Mankind's place. The oceans will calm, less rain will fall, and one day in a thousand years hence when the Giant Upright Rabbit People will find the not completely dissolved remains of a flat-topped yurt-dwelling not far from the overgrown ruins of Woking, they will conclude that, though Mankind had it coming, and was infinitely bad for the planet, one Human was at least wise and lived at one with Nature.

We're all in it together, except for annual leave and Bank Holidays

THE ENVIRONMENT
(WHEREVER THAT IS)

The environment is one of the most important issues facing the world today. The planet is in peril. It is our precious home. Delicate, unique, and it's not our planet it is our children's blah blah blah blah. It all sounds pretty straightforward when you put it like that.

What complicates it, of course, is the likes of Greenpeace, who no one asked but who insist on offering an opinion. If you behaved like that in life you'd end up pissing off a fair chunk of people pretty quickly, but for some reason everyone thinks they're magic. Anyone carrying on like that in my gaff would find themselves on the fast-track to being barred. Butting in, acting holier than thou, and all unsolicited. If there's one thing normal reasonable folk can't stand it's someone who knows they're right, regardless of whether they are or not. No wonder the French sank their boat.

But in recent years the business of the environment has crept into normal politics, and as a result directly affected you and me, demonstrating the Third Rule of **Common Sense** ('How Does It Affect Me?'). Environmental politics used to be called conservation and its patch was worrying about frogs and stuff, putting underpasses in for hedgehogs and so on, and all of that I can appreciate and understand. Anything that means I don't have to repeat the horror of finding a charred hedgehog in the bonfire in the beer garden the morning after Guy Fawkes Night is Good Government as far as I'm concerned.

But the most tangible effect that all this political posing about global warming has had is to put up our gas bills. Which makes me clench my fists when anyone ever mentions Greenpeace.

But, I do understand that saying stuff about the environment is the kind of thing you're meant to do these days. And for that reason it really matters to me that I say the right things too. Now I don't have the money nor do I have the inclination to go hug a husky. I won't live in a yurt or put my own dung in a wood burner, not for my children's generation, nor my children's children's nor for any bastard's children's. I won't sit in my lounge with the lingering smell of burned turd for anyone's future, that's all I'm saying.* Who would? And besides, I'm a fan of proper central heating despite the relentless wearying compromises it demands of us.

*I'm aware that there's no immediate chance of that happening but these Greenies take the thin end of the wedge, that's all I'm saying. And I'm not riding a bike for anybody.

Know this: wherever there is flooding people can rely on me to turn up in wellington boots and stand around looking sympathetic.

If anyone wants to build a runway near where I live I will object. Especially if there's already an airport there. I want some other bastard's neighbourhood ruined, thank you very much.

I am in favour of fracking everywhere except where I live. I've weighed up the data, the economic case, the short- and long-term employment prospects it would bring, the pros and cons. I've carefully read the arguments put by both sides, and what I am worried about is Godzilla turning up where I live and destroying the fracking site and my house to express Mother Earth's disappointed anger at her gaseous virginity being violated.

Now if any of this sounds to you like NIMBYism – Not In My Back Yard-ism – then yes, that's exactly what it is.

Trouble is, you can't encourage a whole country to buy their own places, be proud of them, and rely on the prices of those houses to go up for ever and ever and then expect them to say, 'Yeah, sure, fine, dig up my place, sure, I don't care.' They didn't Think It Through. **Common Sense**.

So some of this environment stuff is walking a fine line.

To this end I want to make some line-walking pledges on the environment:

✗ Pledge to put Boris Johnson on an island. He keeps saying that's what he wants.

✗ By the end of the first five years I pledge it will be five degrees warmer. I reckon the UK could deliver on this pretty easily and it'd mean I didn't have to ring up the Chinese and ask them to knock it on the head, which I can't imagine they either appreciate or listen to. It'll also bring exactly the kind of weather to our coastal holiday towns that successive governments have failed to deliver year on year, aiding economic recovery in some of our hardest hit areas.

✗ Arm all badgers to level the playing field a bit.*

✗ Hunting with foxes to be reintroduced: chickens are vermin.

✗ Jet to global environment summits as much as possible, fly business class, drink as much free booze as possible, fill my boots etc., but do so with a knowing smirk.

✗ Unemployment hamster wheels to meet the gap left by conventional and nuclear power. The millions of people sat around watching Jeremy Kyle are using

* Rock on, Brian!

energy where energy could be produced. Benefits claimants can either live in carbon neutral houses and run on a generator treadmill if they want to watch telly, or come to special energy camps and cover the gap in generator capacity. **Common Sense**.

✘ All wind turbines to be renamed windmills, because that's what they are for Pete's sake.

✘ New technology to be introduced: catching the wind in a great big net perhaps, or something that works with waves maybe, I don't know, we'll get our best people on it.

✘ Rather than fight the flooding in Somerset, turn Somerset into a water park.

✘ Build some houses, but without bringing down the house prices.

✘ Statements about carbon emissions being reduced, will be reduced by 100%.

✘ All utilities to be re-nationalized, apart from the ones I've got shares in.

Because it's not your fault and someone else's problem

A commitment to being fully committed

POLITICS IS ALL ABOUT COMPROMISE:

Sometimes all you need is **Common Sense**, a little lateral thinking, which isn't like thinking, literally.

Wind farms

Wind farms are controversial. They ruin views, harm birdlife. Yet they are the energy solution of the future. **Common Sense** Compromise: **invisible wind farms**.

One man, one job

Millions of unemployed people could be got back to work at the cost of one man's job: Jeremy Kyle's.

It can be clearly linked by **Common Sense** – indeed, it stands to reason – that the *Jeremy Kyle Show*, which is peopled by the unemployed, watched by the unemployed, is actually sustaining and building unemployment.

Shut him down and you will free up millions for work. And even if it doesn't, and even if I am completely wrong, even if what I'm suggesting is based on a piss-poor generalization, you have to admit it's got to be worth trying.

As Dr Spock said in *Star Wars*: 'The needs of the many outweigh the needs of the few.' **Common Sense** solutions. Compromise, Jezza.

The burka

The burka presents us with a dilemma. We are free people, freedom is the very essence of how we live our lives.

That means I can wear what I like, you can wear what you like. Simple.

I can't tell you what to wear, you can't tell me what to wear. That's how it works.

If you want to wear a hoodie in your late forties at no point shall I judge you, call you out for trying to mask your creeping feelings of impotence, insecurity and irrelevance as your youth drains away and your dreams turn to dust: I will not do that. Because it is not for me to say. Or do. Wear what you want. However tragic.

But – and here's the dilemma – we are also a faces people. We like faces. We like looking at each other's faces, getting a good look at each other, that way we can size each other up.

So the burka presents us with a dilemma. A big one. I can't tell you what you want to wear, but I want to see your face. What we need is a compromise. For the sake of community cohesion, we cannot go without a compromise on this matter.

And it's this. You can wear a burka, anyone can wear a burka, whoever they are, whatever the faith. But if you want to wear a burka, what you also have to wear is a **photo of your face**.

Saudi Arabia

Well. Look this one is tricky. But. Oil. Compromise, all right? It's that or fracking.

Equality in the workplace

Oh, do we have to? Women are better than men. Everyone knows that. And that's why they should be paid less, and because they're worth more it's better value to pay them less. Stands to reason. Reckonomics.

Selling arms

Arms sales make some people feel uncomfortable. But there's one simple reply to that: British jobs! British jobs are essential, need taking care of. And rightly so. But, also important is to make sure that if there are people buying weapons they're buying ours, just as long as we keep copies of the manuals.

Expenses

Of course we're all aware it's a terrible scandal that MPs have been abusing our trust by using taxpayers' hard-earned money to subsidize their lavish lifestyles.

However, we have to think of the bigger picture sometimes and imagine the terrible harm that will be done if we pull the plug on the expenses industry. Just think of the duckpond engineers who would find themselves out of a job, out on the street and unable to feed their families. Oh, and please spare a thought for the maître d' in the Dorchester who'd miss out on substantial tips, thus consigning him to a life of untold misery. Sometimes in life it's best to switch on the shredding machine and look the other way.

The World Cup

If we really want to host the 2054 World Cup it would be nice to think we could achieve it with a down-the-line, straight-as-an-arrow, above-the-board bid. However, sometimes in life ensuring you make a small fortune from selling merchandise featuring an official mascot which looks like a cross between a Brontosaurus and a constipated Paul Scholes, takes precedence over fair play. We will have to cast aside our traditional fair-minded attitude and be forced to go in with both feet, studs up, using dastardly Machiavellian tactics such as putting large amounts of money into the offshore accounts of unspecified Fifa delegates. Off the top of my head.

THAT SWING THING
– EVERY VOTE
COUNTS

by Professor Hug Gov, polling expert

Opinion polling is an imprecise science. That's why polling companies differ in their readings in the run-up to an election. Those of us in the polling community are always told that 'everyone remembers 1992', when we apparently got it wrong. Well let me set the record straight.

Firstly, I called it right about a week before and even my mates will back me up on that because I specifically said it when we were in the Wheatsheaf, just before Dave yacked his hoop up on the carpet.

Secondly, I don't remember it because I slipped into a coma the night before the election and only woke up a couple of days later. So there.

I have never wrongly predicted the outcome of an election that I've been conscious for. I even correctly predicted the outcome of the 1955 election despite being just three years old, but that was on a deeply unreliable technique about which boob my mother would breastfeed me from. I've tried to get her to resurrect her old hobby but at eighty-three she's not up to it and keeps calling me a pervert for asking.

The main problem with polling is that British people are liars. I've been lied to my whole life and I'm starting to get sick of it. Mother lied to me about where our pet rabbit had gone. She told me it had gone to a special farm in the sky. She must have thought I was stupid, I knew for a fact that it had gone in the blender because I saw her slit its throat one night when the chippy was closed. It was an insult to be lied to that way by my mother, especially on my thirty-fifth birthday.

It goes further than my family. When I'm polling the public, people openly lie to my face when I'm out in the street with my clipboard. 'Sorry, I'm in a rush,' they'll say, but when I follow them I see them buying a chocolate cake from Greggs before proceeding west through the city centre (not their usual route) and sitting in the window of Giuseppe's Café reading a book. Or a kindle, from the distance I'm at it's sometimes hard to tell. They soon put whatever it is they're reading down once lover boy turns up a few hours later. She's got plenty of time for him, but apparently no time to answer my questions about fish farming. Interesting. I wonder what hubby would make of this? I'm an expert, though, so these hollow deceits don't bother me at all and I don't give them a moment's thought.

EDUCATION

EXAMINING BOARD OF THE BLEEDING OBVIOUS

A-Level Common Sense

Name, you berk: ....

Paper 1

(Please show your working out on the beermat provided)

QUESTION 1

Boiling a kettle

A) Can you boil a kettle?

....

....

B) Why can't you boil a kettle?

....

....

C) Are you some kind of plank?

....

....

QUESTION 2

Boiling an egg

A) Can you boil an egg?

....

....

B) Why can't you boil an egg?

....

....

C) Are you some kind of dipstick??

....

....

QUESTION 3

Changing a lightbulb

A) Can you change a lightbulb?

....

....

B) Why can't you change a lightbulb?

....

....

C) Are you some kind of lemon???

....

....

QUESTION 4

Pulling a pint

A) Can you pull a pint?

....

....

B) Why can't you pull a pint?

....

....

C) Are you pulling my leg????

....

....

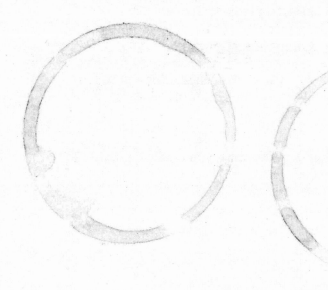

Because it's time for a
quota on quotas

HOW THE EU WORKS

No. 17: Bastards

For hundreds of centuries, the British breakfast has been the envy of the world – the fry-up being widely recognized as one the most iconic icons known to mankind. It's also been scientifically proven by scientists whose job it is to prove things, that it's the best way to start the day. Not to mention the best way to start a case of chronic heart disease, if not eaten in moderation.

However, there's a very large, and very real, dark cloud on the horizon. It's not a cloud full of rain, snow or sleet (I'm using it as a meteorological metaphor) but a cloud full of Brussels red tape which is set to rain on the beautiful British breakfast's parade. The powers that be in the EU have decided that enough is enough and that they want to rob the British people of their birthright – the Great British Fry-up – and replace it instead, with a plate of what can only be described as foreign muck.

Please go online today and help us by signing this e-petition which will probably end up in a civil servant's junk mail, and won't make a blind bit of difference: www.chocolateteapot.com.

What the beautiful British breakfast would look like under proposed EU rules

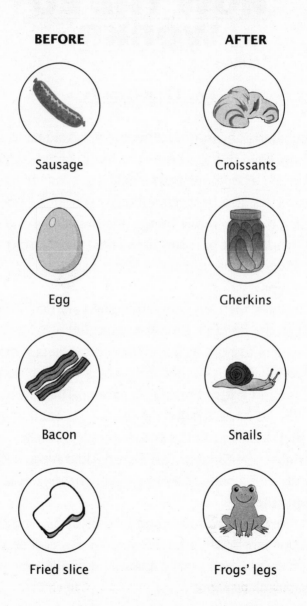

BEFORE | AFTER

Sausage — Croissants

Egg — Gherkins

Bacon — Snails

Fried slice — Frogs' legs

Bubble

Fruit

Beans

Yoghurt

Mushrooms

Granola

Toast

Garlic

Black pudding

Camembert

Buying you a drink with
your money

GREAT BRITONS

NO. 27: THE BBC

The next in our series of Great Britons doesn't
feature a person so much as a thing. That thing
being the British Broadcasting Corporation, or
'Auntie' as it's more fondly known by Terry Wogan,
though I'm not sure it ever quite caught on
actually – renowned worldwide for its respected
Reithian values and an over-abundance of
documentaries about people who work in airports.

However, the BBC also has its critics. There are
those who insist that the corporation is a haven
for lefties, pinkos, Trots, Fifth Columnists and,
perhaps most unforgivable of all in their eyes,
daytime television producers. As someone who's
witnessed the squat figure of Dom Littlewood
pointing his dumpy little finger at dodgy
tradesmen and people on benefits with elasticated
waistlines, I can certainly see their point. He's
daytime, and he's anti the more lively end of the
free market. Commie.

There are those amongst us who argue that
£145.50 for a TV licence is way too steep and that

the Beeb is ripping us all off. We know that *EastEnders* scripts are produced based on the recycled toilet paper model, but apart from that example of cost-effectiveness, how would you find enough revenue to pay for all the documentaries, comedy, news, drama and sport? Perhaps most importantly of all, in the absence of the licence fee, who's going to put their hand in their pocket and make sure Alan Yentob doesn't have to stay in a Travelodge again? Food for thought, indeed. And does anyone nod with their back to camera as well as Alan Yentob? No.

Media experts say that Sky has the BBC firmly in its sights, especially when it comes to sports coverage. One BBC executive was quoted as saying, 'OK, we may not have the rights to cover live Premiership Football, the majority of rugby union, rugby league, Test cricket, T20 cricket, The Big Bash, county cricket, boxing – however, on a positive note, we do have some cross-country running, deck quoits and I'm in a very well-paid job.'

When discussing the BBC, it shouldn't be forgotten that radio has also given us some of the most memorable programmes in the history of broadcasting. An example of this is *The Archers*, which has been going for sixty-five years, and its popularity shows no sign of fading. So many memories – who could ever forget that time so-and-so married thingy who used to work in the combine harvester shop? I have, but there again, I never listen to it. It was costing me too much money, every time I heard the theme tune I smashed the radio into a thousand tiny pieces. Nevertheless millions of people tune in every week and listen to storylines containing such diverse issues as gay life in a rural community, modern agricultural practices and what it sounds like when a man extracts his hand from a cow's arse.

Established in 1967, Radio 1 was at the very heart of an era which was colourful, vibrant and innovative. As a result of advice from our legal team, I'll bring the story right up to date by saying that someone called 'Nick Grimshaw' now presents the breakfast show.

But the thing to remember about the BBC is its devotion to balance. Everyone loves the BBC apart from the people who really hate it. And it's because of this that the BBC is the world's most admired/despised news outlet, regarded all over the world as left wing/right wing and relied on/disregarded as the world's primary/last ever source of news/propaganda, on which every programme is a perfect use/disgusting waste of the licence fee.

VOTER GROUPS

Mondeo Man

In the 1990s, it was a truth universally acknowledged that man in possession of a reasonable income must be in want of a Ford Mondeo. Hence 'Mondeo Man' became the must-woo voter of the 1997 election.

Woomeister Tony Blair set out to seduce Mondeo Man with promises of empty promises, dubious wars and punitive jail terms for owners of the Vauxhall Cavalier. He stormed to victory on a tidal wave of anti-Tory resentment, which he alchemized into anti-politics resentment over the course of his anticlimactic ten-year reign as God's emissary to Britain.

Mondeo Man went back to polishing his hub-caps. Hub-caps never let you down. There are still some examples of Mondeo Man, preserved for posterity in special temperature-controlled cases in the British Museum.

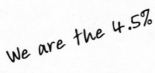

We are the 4.5%

Worcester Woman

'Worcester Woman', another product of the 1990s voting scene, was crucial to Blair's grin-laden 1997 election triumph. Not as crucial as eighteen years of Tory rule and the total breakdown of the Major government, but crucial nonetheless. Worcester Woman was so called because she often underseasoned her cooking and required the addition of a strongly flavoured liquid condiment, and/or was obsessed with the final battle of the English Civil War in 1651, and/or loved traditional English porcelain manufacturers, and/or had tattoos of an early twentieth-century British W-Class destroyer battleship, and/or came from a town or city such as Worcester, and/or was a woman.

Aldi Mum

Not content with stereotyping voters based on their choice of car or location of home, the political classes have more recently condescended their electorate by dumping great swathes of them into an assumed homogeneous electoral wodge based on where they do their shopping. Or, more specifically, where they do some of their shopping.

'Aldi Mum' was launched in 2013, five years into the economic downturn, by the Labour Party, following a successful breeding programme at a secret facility somewhere in the Labour heartlands, in which the femineggs of a Worcester Woman were enspermated with a specimen of love gruel from a Mondeo Man.

Labour's Caroline Flint, the Shadow Energy Secretary and one of the all-party House of Commons Committee for Simplistic Social Groupings, explained at the launch: 'Even though she still buys most things at the supermarket, she probably tops this up with a trip to the local Aldi . . . Aldi Mum is an unashamed bargain hunter who stocks up on the basics at the supermarket but opts for Aldi for the Parma ham and Prosecco wine.'

These touching words showed what desperate, shameful depths of shopping depravity British mums have been reduced to by the economic downturn – buying a small amount of non-vital groceries at a slightly different type of supermarket. Are you listening, 1930s dustbowl America? You don't know how good you had it.

It also shows that Labour are now stereotyping voters not by what they think, nor by what they own, nor by where they live, nor even by where they mostly shop. They are stereotyping them by where they sometimes shop. For a small amount of non-vital groceries. Democracy, the best system there is.

Crawley Man

Launched alongside Aldi Mum, 'Crawley Man' represents the key swing demographic of slightly creepy middle-aged men in suits who try to seduce younger women with a partially convincing air of experience, flattery and dinner. Native to Westminster, but to be found in many constituencies. Not to be confused with Creepy Man. Most likely a One Nation Tory.

Hipster Dad

Not the sort of person you want to admit voting for you, and certainly no one that the likes of Marx or Engels ever conceived of existing, 'Hipster Dad' is the new part of the electorate that has come through in recent years. Hairy yet groomed, modern yet with a taste for old-fashioned trends, Hipster Dad is nevertheless doing his bit for the artisan economy, selling cornflakes at colossal mark-up and reviving the Penny Farthing and spats sectors with much needed injections of cash. Most likely a One Nation Tory, will vote Green out of panic when he gets into the polling booth.

Hospice Gran

The so-called 'grey vote' is crucial at every election, so expect to see the parties fighting false tooth and ingrown nail for the support of Britain's flourishing population of codgers and codgerettes. In close-fought swing seats, nearly dead voters could be crucial, so parties will target 'Hospice Gran' with some aggressive bed-to-bed campaigning during the final days of their and her campaigns. Hospice Gran might be persuaded to vote for a party by promises of a reduction in inheritance tax, a promise that she'll see Albert again on the other side, something to do with the Suez campaign, or more Vera Lynn songs on Radio 2. A One Nation Tory at heart, likely to vote Labour out of pity for that poor boy Ed.

Bus-shelter Uncle

The preventable but unstoppable rising tide of inequality has created a large new constituency of the recently homeless. The supermarket sector has done its best to meet this new demand by slashing the price of higher category street lagers and other forms of 'tramp petrol' and now it is the turn of politics. This portion of the electorate may be cut off from the world of work yet is likely to be well interfaced with the law-enforcement community, and there is every chance – if a fixed abode can be logged when the electoral roll is compiled – that they may well vote for any party planning to cut police numbers. Or indeed a free market, laissez-faire approach to alcohol pricing. Most likely a One Nation Tory.

Oil-Rich Oli

The London-based oligarch might only technically have one vote, but his influence can stretch way beyond that. When not stopping in his house in Knightsbridge he might be found in his place in Mayfair or even his home in Regent's Park. The sheer number of staff 'Oil-Rich Oli' hires means he could influence the vote in these London seats, as well as being able to force house prices up wherever he decides to buy a street of exclusive townhouses. With this kind of power, and a hair-trigger readiness to leave a country if it look like there's a whiff of a chance of taxes going up, Oil-Rich Oli is radioactive in electoral terms. Most likely a One Nation Tory.

Twitter Teen

First-time voters unable to process anything of more than 140 characters in length. LOL. Here's a cat who looks like Hitler. U OK hun? #onedirectionrulez #bantz

PARTY PROFILES
THE BIG TWO

The Labour Party

Very much the comedy outfit of British politics, they might not be taken seriously but in dull political times even the most hard-hearted amongst us has raised a smile at their antics. Just imagine how boring it would all be without Ed Miliband. That man is a walking joke shop. He's got a prank for every occasion, when he can remember to do it.

As we all know, Labour was invented by Karl Marx after meeting the radical feminist Hilary Benn (Tony's mum) at Davos. Despite his name, Marx was a big fan of comedy and decided that Britain needed a political party that wouldn't just get votes but get something far more important – laughs. He set out to create the first sketch-based political party and ever since us Brits haven't been able to get enough of them. If I'm forced to pick my favourite Labour moment I can't so I've picked two.

The miners' strike

Up there with fork handles. Labour loved a good pun and this attempt to get the under-16s out on strike was a brilliant farce. Sadly there are always people who don't get the joke and the NUM mistakenly called their members out on strike, a move that brought about the brutal end of the coal industry in Britain. Entire communities still haven't recovered. Still, those under-16s had a good old chuckle. Apart from the ones who had dads working down the mines, it was quite difficult for them. Arthur Scargill still swears blind that the memo he got said 'Miners' Strike' and not 'Minors' Strike' on it, and that's why he didn't poll his members.

Cash for honours

This was a visionary piece of satire. Back in 2006 paying for anything in cash was ridiculous. We all paid for everything by credit card. (As did the government, it turned out.) Labour planned a sketch that inverted the whole power structure by selling something valuable – a peerage – for something worthless – cash. They say imitation is the highest form of flattery, well we've all ended up imitating it. One of my regulars sold something valuable for cash just the other day, a load of old gold that his grandma left him. It's what she would have wanted. The cash, I mean; it might have helped her have a life-saving operation. Mind you, if she'd known that one of Queen Victoria's private crowns would only fetch £30 she probably wouldn't have killed herself for selling it.

As with any long-running comedy, though, the storylines are getting more and more ridiculous and less and less believable. There's far-fetched and then there's choosing Ed Miliband instead of  David. I can't believe they expected us to fall for that one. Ed Miliband is so committed to dreaming up wacky gags that he now smokes weed for transcendental inspiration. A lot of people have accused me of making this bit up, but think about it. Here are the tell-tale signs that he's mashed out of his swede on bud:

- ✘ He's got dark rings around his eyes and a clogged throat. They can only have been caused by late-night blow-backs and bucket-bongs in the Treasury.
- ✘ The title 'Labour Party Leader' is an anagram of 'Labour Party Dealer'. It's staring you in the face.
- ✘ He appointed Ed Balls as shadow chancellor. The clearest sign of them all. You'd have to be ruined to even contemplate it.

The Conservative Party

The Conservative Party has long regarded itself as the natural party of government in the UK and the electorate has tended to agree. Unlike the Labour Party, with its big issues and grand plans, beliefs and binding clauses, the Tory Party has over the centuries zig-zagged across the political spectrum looking for its true mission, brim-full of purpose but lacking in design, and as a result experimented with a wide variety of approaches.

Victorian reformist One Nation stuff from Disraeli, appeasement from Chamberlain contrasting bulldog resolution from Churchill, Eden's determined efforts to break the British Empire, Macmillan's admirable attempt to do as little as possible, Heath's abject treachery taking the UK into Europe. In government more often than not, as the astute amongst you can tell from that list, the Tories hadn't yet found a unifying theme to underline their work. At least that's how it appears.

Because the truth is they do have a guiding principle: cluelessness. How else can you describe the consistent inconsistency, the lurches left, right and centre and back again?

And then came Mrs Thatcher. A masterpiece of trolling, trolling the left, feminism and her own party, Mrs Thatcher's ascent to power meant the Tories had found their true calling: to break through from being just clueless to being downright nasty. There's no need to go into it in any detail, you know the rest and if you don't it's laid out elsewhere in this book in full mythical terms. The result: the Conservatives appeared to have left behind being clueless to become the 'Nasty Party'.

It wasn't until David Cameron, George Osborne and Theresa May came along that the Conservative Party decided to try to shake off that image. Their effort has mainly consisted of saying that's what they were going to do and then carrying on as normal, throttling babies, putting people on the scrapheap, demanding that the disabled prove they were disabled, waxing fat and taxing tat, but with one notable exception: the introduction of Equal Marriage. For some reason – probably his underlying Tory cluelessness – Cameron seemed to think that the world would owe him a favour if he got this policy through, and that it would mean 'Nasty' was a thing of the past. He could go back to be essentially clueless like his esteemed predecessors.

What he hadn't reckoned with was loyal party members and their unyielding adherence to party principle.

Many members of the Tory Party had, of course, joined the party in the spirit of true cluelessness; furthermore, if you're clueless, nasty isn't too big a leap. In practical terms it's often impossible to tell the difference. But wherever it springs from, the thing about being nasty is it requires being thorough. So what you can't do is be nice to some people or it might mean you start to wonder about slackening off and being nice to other people, and then in the end to everyone. Look: if you're not clueless you'll never understand.

This kind of party discipline, this strict adherence to matters of principle, is one of the things that has kept the Tory Party in power for at least two-thirds of the period since the Second World War. It's admirable. You might marvel at their stiffness, but the anti-Equal Marriage core of the party remained very firm, almost splitting the party, in a way that only the clueless can.

A testament to the party's core values and refusal to worry about what something might look like to other people, this rearguard action in the name of cluelessness can only be regarded as heroic.

'Challenging the Status Quo'nt'

DEAR GUV'NOR SECTION

Mike Spagg,
small-time crook,
Frottingham

Dear Guv,

My next door neighbour, Keith, is a thirty-eighth-generation French immigrant, whose family waltzed over here during the Norman conquest and helped themselves to our British land. Why should he get more benefits than me? I, on the other hand, could probably trace my ancestry back to before the Romans.

Furthermore, I work long, stressful hours handling stolen vehicles for a local mafia boss, whereas Keith lazes around all day on what's left of his backside after being seriously injured in the Falklands more than thirty years ago. Why should I have to subsidize his sedentary, layabout lifestyle through the tax I am unjustly forced to pay on refuelling Luigi's cars?

Keep it sweet.

Mike.

PS I can do you a 1982 Altobelli Causio 3.2 for only £1650 cash.

Dear Mike,

Good question, Mike. Unfortunately, there's still no God-given right and wrong about who should and shouldn't be eligible for benefits, so we have to make it up as we go along. Current prevailing opinion is that, rightly or wrongly, true Brits such as yourself should not take precedence over immigrant stock such as Keith.

And, while successive governments have done everything in their power to financially disincentivize servicemen and servicewomen from (a) joining up in the first place, and more importantly (b) getting injured in combat, (a) many insist on serving the nation's armed forces anyway, and (b) workplace injuries such as Keith's remain an unavoidable occupational hazard for them.

So I'm afraid the rest of us have to dig deep into our wallets for heroes like Keith, even if he hasn't done anything particularly heroic for over three decades. And try to remember – if it hadn't been for the likes of Keith, you would probably be speaking Argentinian by now.

Regarding the tax on fuel, the **FUKP** standpoint is that this should be a matter of personal conscience. If you are not fussed about the environment, or think/know that global warming is a conspiracy cooked up by a few tens of thousands of independent research scientists for slight personal gain, then it stands to reason that you should not have to pay tax on fuel. Your petrol should be cheaper – why should you subsidize the ecological superstitions of others?

Furthermore, if you believe that tax is essentially state-sponsored theft, funding compulsory social engineering, then you shouldn't have to pay the VAT on fuel either. That is the kind of free and fair freedom we all fought all of those world wars for, after all. (And, if you score on both of those 'if's, you probably own several large, gas-guzzling motors, so you would save a sweet wodge of cash. To reinvest elsewhere in the economy, of course.)

If, on the other hand, you love trees and worms for some reason, or would like your hypothetical great-great-grandchildren to be able to do things like breathe, drink and eat – probably, who knows? – then you should be prepared to put your wallet where your conscience is and pay fuel tax. And pay it with a smile on your face.

FUKP calculations suggest that, under this scheme, climate and tax sceptics' tax-free petrol would cost a reasonable and justified 43p per litre. To compensate for this lost revenue, fuel tax would have to be hiked up for those who believe fuel tax should be imposed as a tax on fuel. Their petrol would now cost around £2.97 per litre.

That's a **Common Sense**, fair solution for everyone – personal freedom for those who believe in that fundamental British value, while the greenies and tree-huggers get to devote even more of their money to feeding their environmental hobby horse. It's a **Common Sense**, pay the way you want to pay, put your money where your mouth is, fair solution for Britain.

Cheers,
The Guv

C. Windsor,
Gloucestershire

Dear Landlord,

Has God ever actually saved the Queen?

Regards,
C

The Guv
c/o Thackeray's Brewery
Yellowplush Trading Estate, UK

Dear C,

None of your business. Whether or not our great British Lord has ever had to respond to the words of our wonderful national anthem and save the number-one ranked greatest monarch in the world is neither here nor there. If it has ever happened, neither He nor she – sorry, She – is the sort to bang on about it. But the important thing is that, as long as we keep singing their theme tune, the more likely He is to come up trumps when the big monarch-saving moment comes. Every time it gets sung, God stops whatever He's doing, checks on the monarch, makes sure they're not in any kind of jeopardy, and if they are saves them.

But the fact is, since 'God Save the Queen and/or King' topped the charts on its release in 1745, we have had the three longest reigns by British monarchs in the history of the universe. George III clocked up a cool 59 years 96 days in the hot seat, Queen Victoria's ample royal posterials adorned the throne for 63 years 216 days, and Her Majesty

— 300 —

the Royal Highness Her Gracedness of Majesty Ma'am Queen Elizabeth of All She Surveys II the 5'3" Royal Pocket Rocket is due to overtake Big Vic's record in September 2015.

Furthermore, She is the oldest monarch we have ever had. She is the seventh British monarch to live beyond the age of seventy – all of whom have done so since the national anthem started becoming the national anthem back in 1745.

Coincidence? No. As any half-decent footballer will tell you, when thousands of people are singing a song about you, you raise your game. Since we started singing 'God Save the King and/or Queen', God has clearly got better at saving our Kings and/or Queens. Fact.

Cheers,
The Guv

Alan Scrafe,
Tupperware analyst,
Grovesley

Dear Guv,

I know absolutely nothing about politics, but I love pencils and booths, so I'm going to vote anyway. How should I decide who to vote for? When I bet on the Grand National, I vote on the horsey with the nicest name, or pretty colours. Does that work in elections too?

Alan

The Guv
c/o Thackeray's Brewery
Yellowplush Trading Estate, UK

Dear Alan,

Yes. It's as good a method as any. However you vote, you don't really know what you're getting until after the election, when it turns out they all had their fingers crossed when they promised things like free jelly and ice cream for all children under the age of ninety-five, or tax breaks for the living.

Fair enough, in some ways. After all, you can't spell 'manifesto' without 'if'. So you might as well just pick a candidate or party at random, vote for them, then wait to see what if anything happens if they get in. It is, essentially, not significantly different from picking one after months of careful thought and analysis, and after sitting through weeks of interminable bickering throughout the campaign, and then waiting to see what if anything happens if they get in.

You could also organize an office sweepstake. Put the names of all the candidates in a hat, and whichever one you pull out, you have to vote for.

Cheers
The Guv

Dr Petula Chaughlock,
woman,
Cambridge

Dear Guv,

I know from that advert during the Scottish referendum campaign that women are allowed to vote, but unfortunately aren't very good at it. I am a leading post-doctorate physicist heading a team of researchers investigating the potentially world-changing issue of superconductivity, but also a woman. Can you help me vote please? I don't want to mess it up and embarrass my husband in front of his democracy-loving friends.

Dr Petula

Normal is normal

The Guv
c/o Thackeray's Brewery
Yellowplush Trading Estate, UK

Dear Petula,
Well done for writing in, Petula. It's great that twenty-first century women like you feel able to talk about issues like this, which shows what remarkable social progress has been made in this country. Oh well.

Despite what the make-up of the coalition Cabinet suggests, women are in fact a very important voter group. Men have been voting on stuff for thousands, if not millions of years, whereas women have only relished the heavenly joys of the ballot box for the last century or so.

Nevertheless, rightly or wrongly, ladies' votes – however girlishly cast – count exactly the same as the votes of the more experienced, advanced male voting community. And, I have to say, it's still early days in this Pankhurstian social experiment, but you girls are doing really well – many of you can now even do your vote unaided, as long as you've been given some firm guidelines by your husbands about how to do it.

Like it or not, women's voting is here to stay – and you never know, if you keep trying your best, one day, Britain might even have the unthinkable – a female Prime Minister.

So my advice to you, Pet, would be not to worry too much about who you vote for – it's just great that you're taking part. Concentrate on gripping the pencil firmly, and staying calm in the polling station. After all, you only get one chance to vote every five years, so it is crucial that you do not panic and write a shopping list on your ballot paper, or draw a love-heart instead of an 'X', or cry. You might even find that you enjoy it. Many women do these days.

Cheers,
The Guv

GREAT BRITONS

NO. 73: DAME KATIE HOPKINS

1ST

The words 'legend' and 'icon' are used way too often to describe sportsmen, actors, not to mention various slack-jawed, low-trousered celebrities. Katie Hopkins has never been described thus, and that's the way she'd want it. A role model to the box jellyfish and Italian businessmen from New Jersey, she's a no-nonsense, hard-nosed individual who doesn't stand on ceremony for anyone. Even if she'd just won an Olympic Gold medal for one of the good ones, like the 100 metres.*

If you speak to fellow hard-nosed business people and media figures who also refuse to stand on

*Olympic Sports have to have real world usefulness, I'm sure you agree. 100 metres sprint – 110 yards rather – is running for the bus. Therefore useful. Long jump – getting across a canal. Discus? Nah.

ceremony, toe the line and don't suffer fools gladly, they'll tell you that no one in their rarefied world has a nose quite as hard as hers.

Recently on Twitter she delighted her millions of followers by Tweeting the following hilarious response to someone who had the audacity to say 'Hi!' to her.

 Katie Hopkins
@KTHopkins

How dare you say 'Hi!' you stupid, dish-faced prick. You've got 27 followers and I've got 80,000,043 you sad, lonely little fuck.

Hopkins has insulted most people on Twitter – she famously called God a 'twat' for inventing wasps, Moses a 'dick' for using tablets made of stone instead of A4 and George Washington 'a wanker' for owning up to his dad.

There are those who have accused Katie Hopkins of being a horrendous, ignorant, foul-mouthed oxygen thief – but as someone who doesn't suffer fools gladly, pull punches or stand on ceremony she probably appreciates their candid views. Either that or she's blocked them and reported them to Twitter.

It was as a contestant on *The Apprentice* that Katie Hopkins was first catapulted into the public conscience. Which is a shame, because I don't watch it, and if it were down to me I wouldn't use a catapult for her, I'd make sure she was fired from a cannon into the river Thames.

After that she made what can only be described as a massive impact on *Celebrity Big Brother*. That's a bit of a bummer, because I don't watch that either, and I can't be bothered to get it up on YouTube.

Recently she took part in a social experiment in which she shed every ounce of dignity by gaining weight, in order that she could appear on the television a bit more.

As a journalist she has the ear of the nation – giving it to the *Sun*'s readership with both barrels, shooting from the hip and another clichéd expression involving a firearm which I can't think of at the moment.

However: she performs a valuable function, and for this reason we should cherish her. Often in life making decisions is tough, saying the right thing even harder, seeking out wisdom on the road to enlightenment is nigh on impossible in a busy world. Hopkins shines like a lighthouse or buoy marking a perilous set of rocks, and for that reason we should be grateful.

OTHER FORMS OF GOVERNMENT

Dictatorship: one man one vote

I believe in benevolent dictatorship provided I am the dictator. Richard Branson

Dictatorship is without a doubt the very worst kind of government there is. It sometimes seems like it might work. Certainly when democracy looks like it's running out of steam. Not held back by party politics, the complications of debate and so on: it's one bloke in charge doing whatever he wants, could be a good thing, yeah?

Tempting as it might seem to be, one bloke in charge doing whatever he wants is actually not a good thing. Unless you're that one bloke. In which case I guess it's a great laugh right up until the crowd come for you and hang you from a meat hook by your testicles. And while you're hanging from the meat hook you'd probably try to take your mind off the pain by casting your mind back to the gold taps, the swimming pools, the personal bodyguards who you hand-picked, if you get my drift, the gold pistol with ivory handle, the

Zil limos Stalin sent you and you think, yes it was worth it. Because it'd have to be.

In a democracy you might end up voted out, but very rarely – and usually you'd have to have cocked up properly to find yourself in the vertical strung-up-by-your-knackers situation. The worst you might have to deal with is a disappointing book signing when you bring out your memoirs, and maybe a place on the board of a small utility company rather than one of the big boys. But no knacker stringing.

So that's how a dictatorship ends. But how does it get started? The standard pattern is a top notch charismatic fellow – and it's usually a bloke, often a mid-ranking officer in the army – wins an election, promising hot dinners and your land back. He might even mean it, too. OK so he's waved his pistol about a bit, possibly shot his predecessor, and the election is normally one of those elections involving the odd Kalashnikov, but not too much that's untoward. Five years in and there's another election, a total landslide and the leader of the opposition can't get out of his house for some reason. Broken legs, that kind of reason. All the newspapers love you. And the ones that don't are finding it hard to file copy from prison.

Five years later there isn't an election and Colonel Barry Charisma is Leader for Life. He's got three palaces done, four more under construction, a clinic in

Switzerland where they sort your wife's boobs and will arrange bank manager meetings, the usual. Oh? The public? Well they're dealt with because every now and then when there isn't a toilet paper shortage they get to have a big festival and let off steam. Make sure you give half of them stuff every other year, one tenth of them pistols and a loyal thousand machine guns and the whole thing should run smoothly.

So basically it's a laugh if you're the one man with the one vote, but all good things come to an end. The mob (who your advisers always said loved you, which you always found surprising given how many of them you'd had shot), annoyed with skidding their underpants every single day of their lives and fed up with the rumours of a golden bathtub with running hot and cold blondes, march on your palace – often accompanied by well-meaning Western airstrikes – and hang you up by your nuts.

CONCLUSION: Being a dictator is easily the best form of government if you are the dictator. Apart from the being strung up by the nuts part.

I'm sorry, what was the question, love? You're from the gas board? Do come in. Yes, Harry's pension book is just over there . . .

Valerie Cartilage, 73, retired bottle-cap fitter

THERE'S NO SUCH THING AS SOCIETY

Society exists only as a mental concept; in the real world there are only individuals. Oscar Wilde. Not Thatcher. Makes you think.

Society is falling apart at the seams, families splitting up, blah blah blah, single mums, blah blah, teenagers blah blah really frightening blah blah blah blah envy their youth. You know the score. Standards, family, that's what matters. Blah blah.

Radical effort will be required to turn the clock back on the relentless march of the decay of the fabric of blah blah my parents blah blah who decided blah blah that blah blah makes your blood boil. You know as well as I do I don't need to write anything else. It's an old tune, hum along.

But if we are going to make a difference, make a change and restore the sort of blah blah values blah blah respect blah blah sorry there I go again. Here's what needs to happen.

It's all about family

- ✗ It's time to bring back shame. It's at least two generations since grown men went 'corr' at the thought of a pair of knickers and then blushed. Nowadays there are knickers everywhere, on billboards, on the girl at work leaning over the photocopier. In the old days a glimpse of knickers meant you were go, action stations, up periscope. Now that there's no shame there's knickers everywhere. It's too much. An Embarrassment Tsar will be appointed who will take to the streets as part of our 'Cover yourself up, Britain' campaign.
- ✗ The stocks to be brought back. As a compromise to our friends in the Green Party* only organic fruit and veg to be thrown.
- ✗ Bring back hanging, if only for the sake of the rope industry.
- ✗ The Tory Party's proposal to get rid of the Human Rights Act doesn't go anything like far enough, I think it's time to reclassify the people of the UK as not human. **Common Sense**.
- ✗ A ban on the words bro, chillax, and sweeeeeet.
- ✗ Women breast feeding should cover up: in fact let's go further, anyone bottle feeding should wear a blanket over their heads too. Might offend people who don't like bottles.
- ✗ Underpants go under the trousers, clue's in the name.

---

*I like the Greens. They're honest about legalizing what they've been smoking, That kind of honesty is very refreshing in British politics.

- ✗ And then there's the issue of Aslan. Let's face it, what we are dealing with here is ignorance. These Muslamic Fundamentaloids, these radical followers of Aslan, have no legitimacy. They are nothing to do with Aslan, they do not represent Aslan. *The Lion, the Witch and the Wardrobe* is full of pictures of Aslan. Ignorance is no match for **Common Sense**.
- ✗ And a tax break on ties, I'd like to see the country smarten up.
- ✗ Ban Black Friday. We're not yanks. Have some dignity.
- ✗ The youth of today need to toughen up. Babies will be left out overnight and the ones that make it, make it. Those who don't, don't. It'll free up disabled parking for future generations.

No one said solving society's problems would be easy. In fact the chances are it's going to be really difficult. But if we don't try to make a mess of this, who will?

Standing up for what matters: pregnant ladies and old people

THE OBESITY EPIDEMIC

I'm fat, but I'm thin inside . . . there's a thin man inside every fat man.   George Orwell*

Bloated Britain

We are in the grip, we are told, of an obesity epidemic. People are getting fatter and fatter day in, day out. Kids are entering the next stage of human evolution, in which mankind's legs become useless paddles, their hands good for nothing more than working video games controls or shovelling chips into their hungry gobs.

What to do? Well, I think I have the answer. Any epidemic is best dealt with by prevention rather than cure. Getting someone to stop stuffing their face is an uphill task, so the best thing is to make sure they're not doing it in the first place. Fatty foods, carbohydrates, eggs – these foods seem to be the problem. Exposure to these foods is, we are told by the Doctors, dangerous.

*You have to have an Orwell quote in a politics book, it's the law.

And that is why I have developed a vaccine for the obesity epidemic. Well, I say developed, I have found it in traditional methods. Chips themselves aren't contagious, and mini Kievs are not infectious, as long as you defrost them properly, so what's needed is a form of inoculation. We all know how that works, you trick the body into thinking it has already had the illness by giving it a depleted or reduced form of the threatening bacteria or virus and then your body is able to deal with the virus in its full form. Simple.

Vaccines work

Now it may surprise you that the obesity vaccine is an ancient traditional medicine, one that has been handed down over generations, made in homes every day all over the country. It's an answer that once you know what it is you'll wonder why you ever wondered what it was. Because it's clear as day that the traditional vaccine for the obesity epidemic is a Full English/Scottish/Welsh/Irish/Ulster/local areas may have their own variant Breakfast. Egg, bacon, fried bread, hash browns, sausage, beans, grilled tomato, mushrooms, slice of toast, pot of tea. That way the body is fully protected against any fatty foods you may eat later in the day, any eggs, cholesterol, spuds, meat, fatty foods will then be rejected by your body. **Common Sense**.

Now, as you go on you may find you need to up the dose. If the vaccine isn't at first working and you seem to be putting weight on, the best thing to do is bung on an extra egg (not poached! too healthy), maybe an extra piece of fried bread, another sausage. You may also have a reaction to the vaccine, such as putting on some weight, feeling bloated, sluggish, sweating when climbing stairs: don't panic. That's the vaccine at work. It takes its time, and sometimes the bloatation goes on for many months. It's also worth remarking that this is a flexible, open-ended vaccine: if you are particularly worried about what effect chips might be having on your diet, add them to your breakfast.

'Fighting the obesity epidemic one oven chip at a time'

Putting slogans first

CONCLUSION: ASK NOT WHAT YOU CAN DO FOR YOUR COUNTRY, ASK HOW MUCH YOU CAN GET IN HOUSING BENEFIT

But in the end, my friends, Squires, what is the answer?

What can we do, caught in the teeth of this great big grinding thing, government, media, the sodding lies, dishonesty, the electoral system, this Leviathan, if you will? How can you make head or tail of it? Well, if you've got this far you'll know that **Common Sense** has got your back, **Common Sense** knows just how tough it is to get to grips with a lot of this. **Common Sense** knows just how you feel.

After all, if you sit back and look at it all it can seem like there's every chance that what we do makes no difference. Empires rise and crumble, politicians crash and burn, civilizations collapse. The only reliable –ism in life isn't Capitalism, Communism, Socialism, Fascism, Environmentalism, it's Pessimism. It won't let you down. Life is a series of endless, relentless, grinding disappointments.

Truth is, it's fair to say that the best thing we can all do is get our heads down and get on with it. You can't rely on governments, you have to carve your own course. And when weighing up how to live your life you can do a whole lot worse than turning to the Wisdom of the Ancients.

This is why in the end I always think the best place to look is the ancient wisdom of the greatest thinker the world has ever known, a philosopher unmatched in all human history, a British thinker, a man not as popular as he used to be, a man by the name of Jesus Christ.

Jesus – and this is a Christian country, I think we've covered that already thank you; pipe down, Mr Dawkins, do you really think you're helping, mate? – was a top man. Walked on water, you know. Well, we don't actually, but if your mates are prepared to say that on your behalf you must be someone very, very special. Someone who always got their round in.

And Jesus said many, many wise things. Excellent things. Things to live your life by. Things worth remembering and dwelling upon. Off the top of my head I can remember two of them.

The first is perhaps the most famous thing he said: that you should

'Love your neighbour as you love yourself.'

Beautiful, isn't it? Something to aspire to. Something to aim at. And it's there in all the religions, actually. They call it the Golden Rule. You will have seen it in different forms:

'Do unto others as you would have others do unto you, R2D2.'

That's the Jedi version. It's there in all of them, it's even a tenet of Aslan, it's right there in *The Lion, the Witch and the Wardrobe*:

'I say Timmy, don't be a rotter, you wouldn't like it if someone was a rotter to you now would you? Can I have some jam sandwiches please Mr Beaver?'

I've not read it. Not interested. Unfortunately, thanks to some of its wilder adherents, no one dares quote from it – even the good bits – without worrying about being chopped up or mutilated. Ignorance, that's what we are dealing with here. Ignorance. If making a stand like this makes me a hero, then so be it.

FUKP

**VOTE
FOR THE
GUV'NOR**

However, the thing is, had Jesus really thought it through? Does 'Love your neighbour as you love yourself' really stand the test of time? How does it stand up in 2015, these tumultuous times? Oh, I'm sure in AD30 when he came up with it, it rocked everyone's world, and the twelve chancers with him hanging around for free drinks high-fived him and said, 'Yeah, you've done it again, JC! Nice one!' But the truth is I don't think it does stand up. Take a look at the world in which we live, the world we have made for ourselves.

I'm not sure 'Love your neighbour as you love yourself' does stand up, because I don't think Jesus took into account the invention of Resident's Parking Permits. Because if that bloke from next door parks in my spot, outside my house, that I pay eighty-five quid a year for, I'll gut the bastard.

So much for the Golden Rule. Jesus also said that you should:

'Live each day as if it's your last.'

Now what does that one mean? Well, I think there are two interpretations of this. It either means that what you need to do is sit yourself down and take stock of how your life has gone, look at the things you have done wrong, seek forgiveness from those you have sinned against, forgive those who have sinned against you and in turn forgive yourself and the place to find that forgiveness is in the Kingdom of Heaven blah blah blah blah blah blah blah blah blah blah blah blah blah, amen. In other words, don't let a moment pass you by, don't take anything for granted, don't for one minute imagine that who you are and what you do don't matter.

That's one interpretation. The other is if it's your last day on the planet you might as well get on the grog.

And, no you cannot judge us, for we are British, and it is **the way of our people**.

And remember, whatever life throws at you:

'Ed Balls'.